THE LETTERS OF
MALACHI MALAGROWTHER

A

The Letters of Malachi Malagrowther

Sir Walter Scott

With a preface and essay by
P. H. Scott

WILLIAM BLACKWOOD
EDINBURGH

William Blackwood
32 Thistle Street
Edinburgh EH2 1HA

First published 1981
Preface and essay © Paul Henderson Scott

ISBN 0 85158 142 0

Printed by William Blackwood & Sons Ltd

Contents

Preface

THIS book contains the full text of Sir Walter Scott's *Letters of Malachi Malagrowther*, along with an essay, *The Malachi Episode*, which I wrote for *Blackwood's Magazine* in September 1976. The essay discusses the *Letters*, the circumstances in which they were written and their immediate results.

The *Malachi Letters* were first published in the *Edinburgh Weekly Journal* in February and March 1826 and immediately reissued as a pamphlet by William Blackwood. They have been reprinted in the collected editions of Sir Walter Scott's miscellaneous prose, but they have long been unavailable in a separate and readily accessible form. The purpose of this publication is to meet this need.

The *Letters* dealt successfully (because they forced a change of Government policy) with an issue that was important at the time, the issue of Scottish bank-notes which were then the main form of currency and credit in Scotland. But more than this, they dealt in a way which is still topical with the whole question of the relationship between Scotland and England. They are the fullest expression of Sir Walter Scott's ideas on the subject and his only publication on a political question. They are therefore important for an understanding of his views on a matter which was one of the mainsprings of the best of his works. They also amount to the first manifesto of modern Scottish nationalism.

The Malachi Episode

IN February and March 1826, Sir Walter Scott, breaking, as he said, 'a good and wise resolution' not to write on political controversy, sent a series of three long letters to the editor of the *Edinburgh Weekly Journal* 'on the proposed change of the Currency, and other late Alterations, as they affect, or are intended to affect, the Kingdom of Scotland'. They were at once reprinted as a pamphlet and ran into several editions. They not only provoked a sensation, debates in both Houses of Parliament and a Government-inspired reply; but, and this must be a rare achievement, actually caused the Government to change its policy. These were the letters which Scott, with his weakness for absurd pseudonyms, attributed to *Malachi Malagrowther*, a supposed descendant of Sir Mungo Malagrowther, a character in one of his own novels, *The Fortunes of Nigel*. If the name was facetious, there was no doubt that Scott's purpose was entirely serious. He was concerned not only with the currency question, which was the opportunity and the pretext but much more with the whole problem of the relationship between Scotland and England, on which he had thought long and felt deeply. It is a subject which is still very much with us. The *Malachi Letters* deserve to be rescued from Volume 21 of Scott's

Miscellaneous Prose Works, where they have been hidden for the last hundred years or so in the disguise of ephemeral journalism.

For the Scott bicentenary in 1971, the University of Edinburgh held an important conference at which scholars from many countries read papers on virtually every aspect of Scott's work. As far as I can discover, there was only one reference to Malachi. It was in a paper by Donald Low on 'Periodicals in the Age of Scott'. Dr Low said: *'The Letters of Malachi Malagrowther*, for example . . . reveal that he did not always find it easy to combine his support of the Government with his pride in Scotland. The tone of the letters is that of affronted nationalism and political frustration. Yet these powerful feelings are indulged over a subject of limited significance—disagreement as to whether Scottish banks should be allowed to issue their own bank-notes. Aggressive emotion is diverted from political actuality to an almost irrelevant area of play.' The first two of these sentences make fair points; but the others are radically wrong on two, if not three, counts. At the time, Scottish bank-notes were not of mere symbolic importance, as they may be now, but an essential form of currency and the chief means of credit in Scotland. The question was so politically actual that it provoked an unprecedented response from the whole country. Even so, Scott was concerned more with the wide general implications than with the immediate practical issue alone. All of this is obvious from the *Letters* themselves and from Scott's own comments in his *Journal* and private correspondence. That the only reference in the Edinburgh conference should miss the point so completely shows how far the *Malachi Letters* have been either forgotten or misunderstood.

Scott sat down to write the first *Malachi Letter* on 18th February 1826, and with his usual dispatch (it is forty-two printed pages long) finished it next morning. This was a month, almost to the day, from 'the awful 17th January', when there was no longer any doubt about the collapse of his own financial affairs. The irony was not lost on Scott: 'Whimsical enough that when I was trying to animate Scotland against the currency bill, John Gibson brought me the deed of trust, assigning my whole estate to be subscribed by me; so that I am turning patriot, and taking charge of the affairs of the country, on the very day I was proclaiming myself incapable of managing my own.' The two events, the public and the personal, were connected.

Scott's misfortunes were one incident among thousands in a general crash of the London money market after a period of wild speculation. The Government's proposal which provoked the *Malachi Letters* was a response to this situation. They hoped to impose restraint by forbidding the banks to issue notes of less than £5. This might have been sensible enough in England, where provincial banks had a poor record for stability and issued notes of only local validity. It would have been a disaster in Scotland, where the standing and practice of the banks were quite different, and where their notes financed all economic activity. Scottish bank-notes were so widely accepted and trusted in Scotland that they had displaced gold, which was hardly to be found north of the Tweed. With this system of bank credit, the Scottish economy had been flourishing. Why did the Government want to disregard the difference in circumstances and upset something which was working well? To Scott it was the last straw, the latest in a series of measures 'to change everything in Scotland to an English model', uniformity for the sake of uniformity, whether it was to the benefit of Scotland or not. He regarded this policy as both insulting and dangerous. It had been disturbing him for years. 'I am certainly serious in Malachi if seriousness will do good,' he wrote to James Ballantyne. 'I will sleep quieter in my grave for having so fair an opportunity of speaking my mind.'

In the first *Letter*, Scott goes straight to what was for him the heart of the matter: 'I own my intention regarded the present question much less than to try if it were possible to raise Scotland a little to the scale of consideration from which she has so greatly sunk.' His impression was that Scotland had been falling into 'absolute contempt' because English Ministers no longer felt it necessary to take Scottish opinion into account. They were very cautious, and rightly so, about making any change in their own laws. Towards Scotland, they had indulged in 'experiment and inno- vation at our expense, which they resist obstinately when it is to be carried through at their own risk'. They had acted in accordance with the theory that 'all English enactments are right; but the system of municipal law in Scotland is not English, therefore it is wrong'. There was a 'general spirit of slight and dislike manifested to our national establishments, by those of the sister country who are so very zealous in defending their own'.

It had not always been so. In the first half of the eighteenth century, Scotland had been too dangerous to touch, and 'some thought claymores had edges'. Subsequently, Scotland had been protected from interference by her poverty. In spite of this neglect, or perhaps because of it, Scottish prosperity had increased in a ratio five times greater than the English. Now Scotland had become an 'experimental farm', where English politicians sought to extend the 'benefits of their system, in all its strength and weakness, to a country which has been hitherto flourishing and contented under its own'.

The reference to claymores sounds like a threat. When the *Letter* first appeared, Scott prefaced it, as he was fond of doing, with a verse from an old song. This sounded even more threatening:

'Out claymore, and down wi' gun,
And to the rogues again.'

He dropped this from later editions when he found that it was being taken too literally in Press and Parliament. In fact, he emphatically rejects any thought of force: 'God forbid Scotland should retrograde towards such a state.' No more talk of old military exploits. Rather than this, it would be better to stay in the Union, 'even at the risk of becoming a subordinate species of Northumberland. But there is no harm in wishing Scotland to have just so much ill-nature . . . as may keep her good nature from being abused; so much national spirit as may determine her to stand by her own rights, conducting her assertion of them with every feeling of respect and amity towards England'.

It is only at this point that Scott turns to the bank-note question. He explains the difference in both the banking system and the commercial needs of the two countries, and attacks the absurdity of applying the same measure to both, merely for the sake of uniformity. 'They might as well make a law that the Scotsman, for uniformity's sake, should not eat oatmeal, because it is found to give Englishmen the heartburn . . . The nation which cannot raise wheat, must be allowed to eat oat-bread; the nation which is too poor to retain a circulating medium of the precious metals, must be permitted to supply its place with paper credit; otherwise, they must go without food, and without currency.'

Scott then invokes the Treaty of Union in a passage of Swift-like irony. (He had edited an edition of Swift, and in writing *Malachi* he probably had *Drapier's Letters on the State of Ireland* in mind.) Unless an old man had been dreaming, there was such a treaty and it contained a clause preventing any alteration of Scots Law, 'except for the evident utility of the subjects within Scotland'. If this treaty really existed, it settled the matter.

These are subjects worth struggling for, Scott continues, and the whole of Scotland should rise in protest. In the case of Captain Porteous, the British Government yielded to the voice of the Scottish mob. Surely, they would not show less deference to a

XV

reasonable and temperate remonstrance. He returns again and again to 'evident utility' and suitability to Scotland as the standards by which measures should be judged. 'It would be no reason for planting mulberry-trees in Scotland, that they luxuriate in the south of England. The universal opinion of a whole kingdom . . . ought not to be lightly considered as founded in ignorance and prejudice.'

The first *Letter* was published on 21st February and had an immediate effect. On the 24th, Scott wrote in his *Journal*: 'Malachi prospers and excites much attention . . . The country is taking the alarm; and I think the Ministers will not dare to press the measure. I should rejoice to see the old red lion ramp a little, and the thistle again claim its nemo me impune.' By the 27th, Rosebery was able to tell the House of Lords: 'Men of all parties who had never agreed on any one subject before, were united in this.' To press home the attack, Scott wrote a second *Letter*, published on 1st March. 'I trust to see Scotland kick and fling to some purpose.' The pamphlet edition had to go out uncorrected, and without last-minute additions, to be on the streets of Edinburgh before a public meeting on the afternoon of 3rd March. The meeting was a triumphant success with only one dissenting voice.

In his *Journal*, Scott described the second *Letter* as 'more serious than the first, and in some places perhaps too peppery'. At the start, his language is cool enough, but the temperature rises as he goes on. He begins with tactics. Now that Scotland has been awakened from her 'passive slumber' and 'the heather is on fire', what is the next step? He addresses the Scottish, Irish and

English Members of Parliament in turn. The Scottish members should lay aside distinctions of party and unite against the 'foreign enemy'. They should not take part in any public business until the Government abandons the currency bill, and until then attend the House only when they can conscientiously vote against the Government. He asks the Irish to remember that the disregard of her rights which Scotland was suffering today, Ireland might suffer tomorrow. He proposes a league between Scotland and Ireland for joint defence against any such attempt. Scott then turns to the English. 'We ought not to be surprised that English statesmen, and Englishmen in general, are not altogether aware of the extent of the Scottish privileges, or that they do not remember with the same accuracy as ourselves, that we have a system of laws peculiar to us, secured by treaties.' They will surely withdraw when they realise that they are infringing national right.

So far, Scott has been moderate and even generous; but he does not conceal his feelings when he deals with the wider question of the treatment of Scotland by England. He makes a distinction between the treatment of individuals, which is kind and amicable, and of Scotland, which is jealous, over-bearing and illiberal. The English attitude is 'all that is yours is ours, and all ours is our own . . .

'There has been in England a gradual and progressive system of assuming the management of affairs entirely and exclusively proper to Scotland, as if we were totally unworthy of having the management of our own concerns . . . What are we esteemed by the

English? Wretched drivellers, incapable of understanding our own affairs; or greedy peculators unfit to
be trusted? On what grounds are we considered either
as one or the other?' It was not as though there were
any advantage in 'centering the immediate and direct
control of everything in London ... That great
metropolis is already a head too bulky'. There is
strength in diversity. 'Let us remain as Nature made
us, Englishmen, Irishmen, and Scotchmen, with
something like the impress of our several countries
upon each!'

The third *Letter*, published in the next issue of the
Weekly Journal on 7th March, need not detain us. It is
mainly concerned with the practical difficulty of
replacing the paper currency by gold. Scott himself did
not much like it, and was ready to suppress it, if
Ballantyne agreed. Scott felt that he should have put
these detailed arguments at the beginning; to state
them now was to 'yield up the question, and to fire
from interior defences before the outworks were
carried'. Evidently, Ballantyne did not agree and one
can see why. Even if this *Letter* is something of an
anticlimax after the other two, it is still an unusually
lively treatment of financial and economic questions.

It is evident even from this short summary that the
Malachi Letters amount to a coherent statement of the
philosophy of Scottish nationalism, a set of ideas
which has been gaining ground in Scotland during the
last hundred years or so. This is the doctrine that
diversity is preferable to uniformity and centralisa-
tion; that Scottish national characteristics are valuable
for their own sake and should not be abandoned

B

without good reason; that government should be responsive to local needs and wishes; that the parliamentary and administrative machine in London is overburdened in any case and should refrain from interfering in Scottish affairs. All of these ideas are expressed repeatedly and emphatically in the *Malachi Letters*, and it would be no exaggeration to describe them as the first manifesto of modern Scottish Nationalism.

It is extraordinary, but no one seems to have noticed this, with the possible exception of John Buchan in his admirable life of Scott, published in 1932. At that time, it was too early for anyone to see the contemporary implications of Scott's position; but Buchan saw the value of *Malachi* and realised where Scott stood politically. *Malachi* would repay study, he wrote, both for its 'acute economic thinking' and its 'sane and honourable nationalism'. He described Scott's political faith: 'Its first element was nationalism. He believed firmly in the virtue of local patriotism and the idiomatic life of the smaller social unit. Whenever Scotland was concerned he was prepared to break with his party, with his leaders, and with the whole nobility, gentry, and intellectuality of Britain. "The Tories and Whigs may go be damned together, as names that have disturbed old Scotland, and torn asunder the most kindly feelings since the days they were invented." ' Buchan remarked that Scott's opinions on economics were 'singularly up to date'. This is now even more strikingly true of his views on the status of Scotland.

Even since Buchan's time, historians have over-

looked *Malachi*. In the last thirty years, there have
been three general histories of Scotland on a large
scale. The most recent and most substantial of these,
the *Edinburgh History of Scotland*, does not mention
the *Malachi Letters* at all. G. S. Pryde, in *A New
History of Scotland*, gives them one sentence. Agnes
Mure Mackenzie, notorious among historians for her
robust nationalism, has only two. Two historians[1] of
the nationalist movement as such do no better. Sir
Reginald Coupland has a short passage, but does not
comment on the substance of the *Letters*. H. J.
Hanham has only a footnote. In all of these brief
references, there is no suggestion that Malachi was
anything more than a fuss about bank-notes. The
accepted view is that British chauvinism aroused by
the Napoleonic Wars nearly destroyed the whole idea
of Scotland in the early years of the nineteenth
century. Modern Scottish Nationalism is usually said
to have begun about the middle of the century, at
about the time when the Association for the Vindication of Scottish Rights was formed in 1853. In fact,
virtually all the ideas promoted by the Association had
already appeared in *Malachi*, nearly thirty years
earlier. It is true that Scott stopped short of calling in
so many words for the repeal of the Union; but so did
the Association. The Home Rule campaign began later
as a response to the increasingly active and centralising
role of governments. But there is only a very short
logical step between the arguments of *Malachi* against
London 'management of affairs entirely and exclus-

[1] R. Coupland, *Welsh and Scottish Nationalism* (Collins, 1954).
H. J. Hanham, *Scottish Nationalism* (Faber, 1969).

ively proper to Scotland' and the demand for Home Rule.

Before we go further into Scott's views on the Union, there are one or two theories about his motives in writing *Malachi* which should be considered. There is, first of all, the persistent idea that the *Letters* were fugitive pieces written to please the Scottish bankers. Grierson in his life of Scott blames this theory on John Wilson Croker (of whom more later), who wrote to the Duke of Wellington on 20th March 1826:

> 'Walter Scott, who, poor fellow, was ruined by dealings with his booksellers, and who had received courtesy and indulgence from the Scotch bankers, thought himself bound in gratitude to take the field for them, which he did in a series of clever but violent and mischevious letters.'

But this letter only became known when Croker's correspondence was published in 1884. Before then, Cockburn had made virtually the same point in his *Memorials*: 'Scott, tempted by the bankers, came forward . . . in the new character of a political pamphleteer. Poets may be excused for being bad political economists.' The whole passage is, for Cockburn, strangely ungenerous. He contrives to celebrate the popular response ('It was really refreshing to see the spirit with which the whole land rose as one man') without giving Scott any of the credit. Presumably the Whig reformer did not like to see the Tory Scott assuming the leadership of a popular agitation.

Grierson could have found his source still further back, in Lockhart and in Scott's own *Journal*. In his biography, Lockhart suggested that three motives were involved in *Malachi*, but not all of equal value:

'Scott, ever sensitively jealous as to the interference of English statesmen with the internal affairs of his native kingdom, took the matter up with as much zeal as he could have displayed against the Union had he lived in the days of Queen Anne. His national feelings may have been somewhat stimulated, perhaps, by his deep sense of gratitude for the generous forbearance which several Edinburgh banking-houses had just been exhibiting toward himself; and I think it need not be doubted, moreover, that the splendida bilis which, as the Diary shows, his own misfortunes had engendered, demanded some escape-valve.'

On 22nd February, Scott referred in his *Journal* to the republication of the first *Letter* as a pamphlet: 'The Banks are anxious to have it published. They were lately exercising lenity towards me, and it will be an instance of the "King's errand lying in the cadger's gate".' In other words, he did not write to please the banks, but if the *Letters* were incidentally agreeable to them, so much the better. There is plenty of evidence in the *Journal* that so far from expecting to advance his personal interests by the *Letters*, Scott knew from the start that he was putting them at risk. He expected to offend his friends in high places in England, which apart from anything else might damage the prospects of his son, Charles. When Lockhart wrote from London to say that indeed 'the ministers are sore beyond imagination', Scott's reaction was to write the second and stronger *Malachi*. He did not expect gratitude even from the bankers: 'But I foresaw it from the beginning. The bankers will be persuaded that it is a squib which may burn their own fingers, and will curse the poor pyrotechnist that compounded it.'

Later biographers have followed Lockhart in speaking of the therapeutic, escape-valve, effect of the *Letters* in allowing Scott to demonstrate that he had not been defeated by his misfortunes. Again, there is supporting evidence in the *Journal* and correspondence: 'On the whole, I am glad of this brulzie, as far as I am concerned; people will not dare talk of me as an object of pity—no more "poor-manning".' But this too was a secondary consequence, not the motive, for writing the *Letters*. 'The impulse,' as Herbert Grierson said, 'came from a deeper source.' On this point, the evidence leaves no room for doubt. The deeper source emerges clearly in his letters to his closest friends. To Lockhart: 'What reason on earth can I have to affront all my friends in power but the deep consciousness that there is a duty to be discharged?' To James Ballantyne (in words already quoted, and they are words which clearly speak deep feeling): 'I will sleep quieter in my grave for having so fair an opportunity of speaking my mind.' To Lockhart again: 'My heart will not brook . . . to leave the cause of my country . . . in a state so precarious without doing whatever one poor voice can to sound the alarm.' This duty, this compulsion to speak, arose from, in

Lockhart's words, Scott's 'national feelings'.

These feelings were both strong and complex. One element was a deep regret for the Scottish characteristics which had already been lost because of the influence of England, and a fear that this process would continue implacably. This was the impulse behind most of Scott's best work. It could make him, as little else could, drop the outward composure of the Edinburgh lawyer and Man of the Enlightenment. Take one example from Lockhart. In 1806, when Scott was thirty-five, he had been opposing certain proposals for change in the procedure of the Scottish courts at a meeting in the Faculty of Advocates. Lockhart continues:

'. . . when the meeting broke up, he walked across the Mound, on his way to Castle Street, between Mr Jeffrey and another of his reforming friends, who complimented him on the rhetorical powers he had been displaying, and would willing have treated the subject-matter of the discussion playfully. But his feelings had been moved to an extent far beyond their apprehension: he exclaimed, "No, no—'tis no laughing matter; little by little, whatever your wishes may be, you will destroy and undermine, until nothing of what makes Scotland Scotland shall remain." And so saying, he turned round to conceal his agitation—but not until Mr Jeffrey saw tears gushing down his cheek—resting his head until he recovered himself on the wall of the Mound. Seldom, if ever, in his more advanced age, did any feelings obtain such mastery.'

There is also the other well-known passage in the introduction to the *Minstrelsy of the Scottish Border*, which shows that Scott approached ballads and bank-notes in something of the same spirit:

'By such efforts, feeble as they are, I may contribute something to the history of my native country; the peculiar features of whose manners and character are daily melting and dissolving into those of her sister and ally. And, trivial as may appear such an offering to the Manes of a kingdom, once proud and independent, I hang it upon her altar with a mixture of feelings which I shall not attempt to describe.'

In addition to this feeling about Scotland, although perhaps to some extent as a rationalisation of it, Scott argued that all change should be approached with caution. 'Hasty and experimental innovations', he says in the first of the *Malachi Letters*, were liable to have 'unforseen and unprovided for consequences'. At the same time, he was ready to admit that change could often be beneficial. He was receptive, in the spirit of the Scottish Enlightenment, to technological improvement. As Virginia Woolf noticed, Abbotsford was one of the first houses to be lit by gas. Perhaps simply because he was a lawyer himself, or perhaps because he thought that changes in the law were liable to have more complex and unpredictable effects, he was more anxious about legislation than technology. Above all, he was worried about the effect on social stability of the loss of traditional values and ideas. He developed this thought mainly in letters to Lockhart and Croker, where he suggested that the erosion of the Scottish identity would disturb people and provoke a destructive, revolutionary spirit, which would make Scotland a dangerous neighbour. This was the sense of the celebrated remark in a letter to Croker: 'If you unscotch us, you will find us damned mischievous Englishmen.'

Of course, Scott's attitude to change has affinities with political conservatism and defence of class interest. In the last year of his life, when he was worn out by overwork and illness, his panic reaction to the Reform Bill looked very much like a simple response of that kind. Normally he was pulled in opposing directions. His emotional Jacobitism and regret for Scotland's turbulent and feudal past were balanced by respect for Hanoverian peace and progress, his Toryism by affection for the common man, even his nationalism by impulses of anti-Napoleonic British chauvinism. As someone has said, the Last Minstrel was also the first Chairman of the Edinburgh Oil-Gas Board. The appropriate reaction to change, the resolution of conflict, were the constant preoccupations of both the Enlightenment and of the major Waverley novels. These conflicts, between the emotional and the rational, the romantic and the Augustan, the past and the future, were involved in almost everything that Scott thought and wrote. No simple, unqualified statement about any of his attitudes is therefore likely to be found adequate. Scott himself was perfectly conscious of the tension: 'It is difficult to steer betwixt the natural impulse of one's national feelings setting in one direction, and the prudent regard to the interests of the empire and its internal peace and quiet, recommending less vehement expression. I will endeavour to keep sight of both. But were my own interests alone concerned, d—n me but I would give it them hot!'

Scott's attitude to the Union is no exception, and no less subject to internal conflict. Strangely enough, a tradition has grown up, repeated uncritically from writer to writer, and bolstered by selective quotation, that this is one case where Scott's views were simple, definite, and all of one piece. This accepted wisdom is paradoxical: that Scott was at the same time an intense Scottish patriot and a strong supporter of the Union. Both Coupland and Hanham say as much, although with very little in the way of supporting evidence. Often Baillie Nicol Jarvie is called as a witness, as if Scott's opinions could be deducted from the words of one of his characters: ' "Now, since St Mungo catched herrings i' the Clyde, what was ever like to gar us flourish like the sugar and tobacco trade? Will onybody tell me that, and grumble at the treaty that opened us a road west-awa' yonder?" ' Andrew Fairservice's reply is less frequently mentioned: ' "It was an unco change to hae Scotland's laws made in England; and that for his share, he wadna for a' the herring-barrels in Glasgow, and a' the tobacco-casks to boot, hae gien up the riding o' the Scot's Parliament . . . What wad Sir William Wallace, or auld Davie Lindsay, hae said to the Union, or them that made it?" ' Or, for good measure, Mrs Howden in the *Heart of Midlothian*: ' "When we had a king, and a chancellor, and Parliament o' our ain, we could aye peeble them wi' stanes when they werena gude bairns—But naebody's nails can reach the length o' Lunnon." '

David Daiches suggested recently that 'where Scott thought he stood on this question in the last part of his life' can be seen in the first chapter of his *Tales of a Grandfather*, where he speaks of 'this happy union'. Scott's views are set out much more explicitly in the three chapters (60-62) which deal with the negotiation of the Union and its consequences. Once again, Scott's feelings break through the even tenor of his prose. The English were 'more desirous to subdue Scotland than to reconcile her', and insisted on an incorporating union. 'The Parliament of Scotland was bribed with public money belonging to their own country.' Phrase piles on phrase: 'The total surrender of their independence, by their false and corrupt statesmen; degradation of their country; loss and disgrace to be sustained by the ancient kingdom which had so long defended her liberty and independence against England.' It all sounds as though Scott was much more in sympathy with Andrew Fairservice than with the Baillie. In fact, his account of the Union in these three chapters suggests very clearly that, like the Scottish negotiators, he would have preferred a 'federative union' with Scotland retaining 'her rights as a separate Kingdom, making as heretofore her own laws, and adopting her own public measures, uncontrolled by the domination of England'. As it was, he thought that 'the interests of Scotland were considerably neglected in the Treaty of Union', although 'all leagues or treaties between nations, which are designed to be permanent, should be grounded not only on equitable, but on liberal principles'. Scott conceded that the Union had 'beneficial effects' in the 'happy change from discord to friendship', and in opening the English colonies to Scottish trade; but these advantages might have been obtained by federation instead of union. He began the *Tales* about a year after *Malachi*, and the two are consistent. He accepted the Union, with regret, in the political conditions of his own time, but hoped that interference in Scottish affairs could be restricted. This was not unrealistic at a time when the activity of governments was very limited.

One of the most revealing sentences in *Malachi* is in the passage where Scott abjures the use of force: 'We do not want to hear her prate of her number of millions of men, and her old military exploits. We had better remain in union with England, even at the risk of becoming a subordinate species of Northumberland, as far as national consequence is concerned, than remedy ourselves by even hinting the possibility of a rupture.'[2] In other words, Scott disliked the Union, but he disliked violence even more. Certainly, his romantic imagination was stirred by the panoply of war. He was never happier than when he was charging on Portobello sands in the guise of dragoon, and his vocabularly ran easily to military metaphors, as in *Malachi* itself. But if this was one of his conflicts, it was one that was firmly resolved. He was too much of a

[2] This sentence was quoted inaccurately by Professor Trevor-Roper in *The Times* (28th April 1976) to suggest that it showed that Scott was opposed to Scottish independence. It is obvious to anyone who reads the whole paragraph that it was violence, not independence, which Scott was rejecting.

realist, and too knowledgeable an historian, to imagine that any good could come of force. Again and again in the *Tales*, he stresses the virtue of the Union in ending conflict between the two countries. To him, this was its greatest merit. Again, this arose from the circumstances of his time. He had talked to men who had taken part in the 'Forty-five, and he had lived through the period of the French Revolution. The possibility of violence between Scotland and England, or that political agitation could turn to extremity and bloodshed, were very real to him. They affected his reaction both to talk of Reform and to the Union. In the pre-Reform House of Commons, there was no possibility at all that the Union could be modified or repealed by constitutional means. Agitation against it was therefore bound to turn to frustration and perhaps to violence. In these circumstances, the only prudent course was to accept the Union as an accomplished fact. This is Scott's predominant attitude, even if he also wanted Scotland to show enough national spirit to assert her own rights. At the same time, he drew attention to such safeguards as the Treaty of Union contained for Scottish rights and interests and argued, both ironically and explicitly, that they should be respected.

Political argument, and political compromise, apart, Scott contributed to Scottish national feeling even more powerfully by the effect of his imaginative writing. No one has ever doubted or disputed this. He created an image of the Scottish past which welded the Highlands and Lowlands together in a heightened national consciousness, and made the rest of the world aware of it for the first time. This is something quite different from the pamphleteering of *Malachi Malagrowther*; but there was a common impulse behind both.

By a curious coincidence, the idea of writing the *Tales of a Grandfather* was suggested to Scott by the example of a similar book about English history by the very man who was chosen by the Government to reply to *Malachi*. This was John Wilson Croker, a sort of latter-day Pepys, who was Secretary of the Admiralty for twenty-two years and a protégé of Wellington. He attracted notice in 1809, when he was twenty-nine and a new Irish member of the Commons, with a poem on the Battle of Talavera in the metre used by Scott in *Marmion*. Scott congratulated him by letter and in a review in the *Quarterly*. From then onwards, Scott and Croker kept up a close and friendly correspondence. It was to Croker that Scott turned when he wanted the permission of the Prince Regent to search for the Scottish Regalia. When Croker was working on an edition of Boswell, Scott supplied him with anecdotes which have now become part of the Johnston legend. Croker was therefore presented with a difficult conflict of loyalties when the Government asked him, as the ablest controversialist at its disposal, to reply to *Malachi*. He acquitted himself with dexterity. His pseudonym, Edward Bradwardine Waverley, was ingenious in itself by implying the reconciliation in his own person of the sympathetic Englishman and the true Scot. It enabled him to make a distinction between *Malachi* and Scott, 'their common parent', and play one off against the other. But his

reply to Scott was a *dialogue des sourds*. He started with such opposed assumptions that he hardly came into contact with Scott's arguments at all. He accused Scott of a 'radical error' right from the title-page, which referred to the Kingdom of Scotland. Croker wrote: 'If Scotland were indeed a Kingdom—a separate and independent sovereignty—the question of uniformity and assimilation might be open to some, though certainly not to all, the observations you make.' At the same time, Croker wrote to Scott to assure him that his personal friendship was undiminished, and Scott replied in the same spirit. He had been tempted to hit back, but would not 'endanger the loss of an old friend for a bad jest'.

Scott objected more to a letter written 'at' him by his still older friend, Lord Melville, who, as the Minister responsible for Scottish affairs, felt himself to be the chief target of *Malachi*. Scott's objection was not so much to the content as to the procedure. Melville wrote to his kinsman and Scott's colleague in the Court of Session, Sir Robert Dundas, and asked him to show the letter to Scott—without giving him a copy—and to other Party friends in Scotland. To Scott this seemed, in Johnson's phrase, 'a sign to hate'. The letter itself accused *Malachi* of an 'inflammatory tendency . . . gross misrepresentation', and 'insulting taunts and unfounded attacks on the present government'; but it did admit that the arguments on the Scottish banks and paper currency were 'very much to the purpose, and deserving of great consideration'. In his reply, Scott admitted that some passages in *Malachi* ought perhaps to have been modified, 'but I desired to make a strong impression, and speak out, not on the currency question alone, but on the treatment of Scotland generally . . . So much for my Scottish feelings—prejudices, if you will; but which were born, and will die with me'.

In the passage in his *Memorials* about the *Malachi* affair, Cockburn says that Scott 'was mentioned in Parliament by his own friends with less respect than one would ever wish to be shown him'. *Hansard* and the Press reports of the time, although admittedly neither is verbatim, suggest that the references were in fact very decorous. Several members criticised Scott on a vulnerable point, his imprudent reference to claymores (although, strangely enough, no one seems to have reacted to his still more provocative phrase, 'foreign enemy'). 'The cry of alarm—the call to resistance—could not have been greater . . . there had been some mention . . . of the claymore,' said a Mr Tierney. But talk of this kind was put in a more sober light by Robinson, the Chancellor, in his Budget speech: 'I shall look without terror on the flashing of the Highland Claymore, though it be evoked from its scabbard by the incantations of the first magician of the age.' This mingling of criticism and praise is typical of both Parliamentary and Press response.

Scott's prestige was so great that he could not be ignored, and anything that he wrote had to be treated with respect. There would have been agitation against the currency proposals in any case. The first of the petitions against them reached Parliament even before the publication of the first *Letter*; but they became a flood afterwards—from every town and county in

Scotland. Faced with such an outcry, and such an opponent, the Government responded quickly. On 16th March, it set up a committee to consider the question, and two months later it was decided to accept its verdict and 'not meddle with the currency of Scotland'. 'The principles, if not the reasoning, of *Malachi Malagrowther* have triumphed . . . and are "crowned with complete success," ' said the *Edinburgh Weekly Journal*. Despite Cockburn, no one at the time seems to have had any doubt that the credit was due to Scott. *The Scotsman* in its report of the protest meeting in Edinburgh on 3rd March quoted a speaker: 'The gratitude of the country was due to him if ever gratitude was due to any man,' and added: 'Great applause—all looking towards Sir Walter Scott.' Even the editor of Croker's papers, L. J. Jennings, concludes: 'In the end, the Ministry withdrew its scheme, so far as it applied to Scotland, and the victory rested with the author of *Waverley*.'

And what of the reaction of Scott himself to this famous victory? Lockhart in the Conclusion of his biography says: 'Whenever Scotland could be considered as standing separate on any question from the rest of the empire, he was not only apt, but eager to embrace the opportunity of again rehoisting, as it were, the old signal of national independence; and I sincerely believe that no circumstance in his literary career gave him so much personal satisfaction as the success of *Malachi Malagrowther's Epistles*.' He might have quoted chapter and verse from Scott's own *Journal*. He refers to an increase in the number of appeals from the Scottish courts to the House of Lords and he concludes: 'The consequence will in time be, that the Scottish Supreme Court will be in effect situated in London. Then down fall—as national objects of respect and veneration—the Scottish Bench, the Scottish Bar, the Scottish Law herself, and—"there is an end of an auld sang". Were I as I have been, I would fight knee-deep in blood ere it came to that. But it is a catastrophe which the great course of events brings daily nearer . . . I shall always be proud of *Malachi* as having headed back the Southron, or helped to do so, in one instance at least.'

A LETTER.

TO THE

Editor of the Edinburgh Weekly Journal,

FROM

MALACHI MALAGROWTHER, Esq.

ON THE

PROPOSED CHANGE OF CURRENCY,

AND

OTHER LATE ALTERATIONS,

AS THEY AFFECT, OR ARE INTENDED TO AFFECT,

THE

KINGDOM OF SCOTLAND.

Ergo, Caledonia, nomen inane, Vale!

FOURTH EDITION.

EDINBURGH:

Printed by James Ballantyne and Company,

FOR WILLIAM BLACKWOOD, EDINBURGH: AND

T. CADELL, STRAND, LONDON.

1826.

A LETTER

ON THE

PROPOSED CHANGE OF CURRENCY.

———

TO THE EDITOR

OF THE EDINBURGH WEEKLY JOURNAL.

My dear Mr Journalist,

I am by pedigree a discontented person, so that you may throw this letter into the fire, if you have any apprehensions of incurring the displeasure of your superiors. I am, in fact, the lineal descendant of Sir Mungo Malagrowther, who makes a figure in the Fortunes of Nigel, and have retained a reasonable proportion of his ill luck, and, in consequence, of his ill temper. If, therefore, I should chance to appear too warm and poignant in my observations, you must impute it to the hasty and peevish humour which I derive from my ancestor. But, at the same time, it often happens that this disposition leads me to speak useful, though unpleasant truths, when more prudent men hold their tongues and eat their pudding. A lizard is an ugly and disgusting thing enough ; but, methinks, if a lizard were to run over my face and awaken me, which is said to be their custom when they observe a snake approach a sleeping person, I should neither scorn his intimation, nor feel justifiable in crushing him to death, merely because he is a filthy little abridgement of a crocodile. Therefore, " for my love, I pray you, wrong me not."

I am old, sir, poor, and peevish, and, therefore, I may be wrong ; but when I look back on the last fifteen or twenty years, and more especially on the last ten, I think I see my native country of Scotland, if it is yet to be called by a title so discriminative, falling, so far as its national, or rather, perhaps, I ought now to say its *provincial*, interests are concerned, daily into more absolute contempt. Our ancestors were a people of some consideration in the councils of the empire. So late as my own younger days, an English minister would have paused, even in a favour-

ite measure, if a reclamation of national rights
had been made by a Member for Scotland, supported, as it uniformly then was, by the voice of
her representatives and her people. Such ameliorations in our peculiar system as were thought
necessary, in order that North Britain might
keep pace with her Sister in the advance of improvement, were suggested by our own countrymen, persons well acquainted with our peculiar system of laws, (as different from those of
England as from those of France,) and who
knew exactly how to adapt the desired alteration to the principle of our legislative enactments, so that the whole machine might, as
mechanics say, work well and easily. For a
long time, this wholesome check upon innovation, which requires the assimilation of a proposed improvement with the general constitution of the country to which it has been recommended, and which ensures that important
point, by stipulating that the measure shall ori-
ginate with those to whom the spirit of the
constitution is familiar, has been, so far as Scotland is concerned, considerably disused. Those

who have stepped forward to repair the gradual failure of our constitutional system of
law, have been persons that, howsoever qualified in other respects, have had little farther
knowledge of its construction, than could be acquired by a hasty and partial survey, taken just
before they commenced their labours. Scotland
and her laws have been too often subjected to
the alterations of any person who chose to found
himself a reputation, by bringing in a bill to
cure some defect which had never been felt in
practice, but which was represented as a fright-
ful bugbear to English statesmen, who, wisely
and judiciously tenacious of the legal practice
and principles received at home, are propor-
tionally startled at the idea of any thing abroad
which cannot be brought to assimilate with them.

The English seem to have made a compromise with the active tendency to innovation,
which is one great characteristic of the day.
Wise and sagacious themselves, they are ner-
vously jealous of innovations in their own laws
—*Nolumus leges Angliæ mutari*, is written on
the skirts of their judicial robes, as the most

sacred texts of Scripture were inscribed on the phylacteries of the Rabbis. The belief that the Common Law of England constitutes the Perfection of human reason, is a maxim bound upon their foreheads. Law Monks they have been called in other respects, and like Monks they are devoted to their own Rule, and admit no question of its infallibility. There can be no doubt that their love of a system, which, if not perfect, has so much in it that is excellent, originates in the most praiseworthy feelings. Call it if you will the prejudice of education, it is still a prejudice honourable in itself, and useful to the public. I only find fault with it, because, like the Friars in the Duenna monopolizing the bottle, these English Monks will not tolerate in their lay-brethren of the North the slightest pretence to a similar feeling.

In England, therefore, no innovation can be proposed affecting the administration of justice, without being subjected to the strict inquiry of the Guardians of the Law, and afterwards resisted pertinaciously until time and the most mature and reiterated discussion shall have proved its utility, nay, its necessity. The old saying is still true in all its points—Touch but a cobweb in Westminster-Hall, and the old spider will come out in defence of it. This caution may sometimes postpone the adoption of useful amendments, but it operates to prevent all hasty and experimental innovations ; and it is surely better that existing evils should be endured for some time longer, than that violent remedies should be hastily adopted, the unforeseen and unprovided-for consequences of which are often so much more extensive than those which had been foreseen and reckoned upon. An ordinary mason can calculate upon the exact gap which will be made by the removal of a corner-stone in an old building ; but what architect, not intimately acquainted with the whole edifice, can presume even to guess how much of the structure is, or is not, to follow ?

The English policy in this respect is a wise one, and we have only to wish they would not insist upon keeping it all to themselves. But those who are most devoted to their own religion, have least sympathy for the feelings of dissenters ; and a spirit of proselytism has of late shown itself in England for extending the benefits of their system, in all its strength and weakness, to a country, which has been hitherto flourishing and contented under its own. They adopted the conclusion, that all English enactments are right; but the system of municipal law in Scotland is not English, therefore it is wrong. Under sanction of this syllogism, our rulers have indulged and encouraged a spirit of experiment and innovation at our expense, which they resist obstinately when it is to be carried through at their own risk.

For more than one half of last century, this was a practice not to be thought of. Scotland was during that period disaffected, in bad humour, armed too, and smarting under various irritating recollections. This is not the sort of patient for whom an experimental legislator chooses to prescribe. There was little chance of making Saunders take the patent pill by persuasion—main force was a dangerous argument, and some thought claymores had edges.

This period passed away, a happier one arri-

ved, and Scotland, no longer the object of terror, or at least great uneasiness, to the British Government, was left from the year 1750
under the guardianship of her own institutions,
to win her silent way to national wealth and
consequence. Contempt probably procured for
her the freedom from interference, which had
formerly been granted out of fear ; for the
medical faculty are as slack in attending the
garrets of paupers as the caverns of robbers.
But neglected as she was, and perhaps *because*
she was neglected, Scotland, reckoning her progress during the space from the close of the
American war to the present day, has increased
her prosperity in a ratio more than five times
greater than that of her more fortunate and
richer sister. She is now worth the attention of
the learned faculty, and God knows she has had
plenty of it. She has been bled and purged,
spring and fall, and *talked* into courses of physic,
for which she had little occasion. She has been
of late a sort of experimental farm, upon which
every political student has been permitted to try
his theory—a kind of common property, where

every juvenile statesman has been encouraged to make his inroads, as in Morayland, where, anciently, according to the idea of the old Highlanders, all men had a right to take their prey —a subject in a common dissecting-room, left to the scalpel of the junior students, with the degrading inscription,—*Fiat experimentum in corpore vili.*

I do not mean to dispute, sir, that much alteration was necessary in our laws, and that much benefit has followed many of the great changes which have taken place. I do not mean to deprecate a gradual approach to the English system, especially in commercial law. The Jury Court, for example, was a fair experiment, in my opinion, cautiously introduced as such, and placed under such regulations as might best assimilate its forms with those of the existing Supreme Court. I beg therefore to be considered as not speaking of the alterations themselves, but of the apparent hostility towards our municipal institutions, as repeatedly manifested in the course of late proceedings, tending to force and wrench them into a similarity with those of England.

The opinions of our own lawyers, nay, of our

Judges, than whom wiser and more honourable
men never held that high character, have been,
if report speaks true, something too much neglected and controlled in the course of these important changes, in which, methinks, they ought
to have had a leading and primary voice. They
have been almost avowedly regarded not as persons the best qualified to judge of proposed innovations, but as prejudiced men, determined to
oppose them right or wrong. The last public
Commission was framed on the very principle,
that if Scotch Lawyers were needs to be employed, a sufficient number of these should consist of
gentlemen, who, whatever their talents and respectability might be in other respects, had been
too long estranged from the study of Scottish law,
to retain any accurate recollection of an abstruse
science, or any decided partiality for its technical
forms. This was done avowedly for the purpose
of evading the natural partiality of the Scottish
Judges and practitioners to their own system ;
that partiality, which the English themselves hold
so sacred a feeling in their own Judges, and Coun-
sel learned in the law. I am not, I repeat, com-
plaining of the result of the Commissions, but

of the spirit in which the alterations were undertaken. Unquestionably much was done in brushing up and improving the old machinery of Scottish Law Courts, and in making it move more rapidly, though scarce, I think, more correctly than before. Dispatch has been much attended to. But it may be ultimately found, that the time-piece which runs fastest does not intimate the hour most accurately. At all events, the changes have been made and established—there let them rest. And had I, Malachi Malagrowther, the sole power to-morrow of doing so, I would not restore the old forms of judicial proceedings ; because I hold the constitution of Courts of Justice too serious matters to be put back or forward at pleasure, like a boy's first watch, merely for experiment's sake.

What I *do* complain of is the general spirit of slight and dislike manifested to our national establishments, by those of the sister country who are so very zealous in defending their own ; and not less do I complain of their jealousy of the opinions of those who cannot but be much better acquainted than they, both with the merits and deficiencies of the system, which hasty and

imperfectly informed judges have shown themselves so anxious to revolutionize.

There is no explanation to be given of this but
one—namely, the entire conviction and belief of
our English brethren, that the true Themis is
worshipped in Westminster Hall, and that her
adorers cannot be too zealous in her service;
while she, whose image an ingenious artist has
depicted balancing herself upon a *te-totum* on the
southern window of the Parliament House of
Edinburgh, is a mere idol,— Diana of Ephe-
sus,—whom her votaries worship, either because her shrine brings great gain to the crafts-
men, or out of an ignorant and dotard super-
stition, which induces them to prefer the old
Scottish *Mumpsimus* to the Modern English
Sumpsimus. Now, this is not fair construction
in our friends, whose intentions in our behalf,
we allow, are excellent, but who certainly are
scarcely entitled to beg the question at issue
without inquiry or discussion, or to treat us as
the Spaniards treated the Indians, whom they
massacred for worshipping the image of the
Sun, while they themselves bowed down to that
of the Virgin Mary. Even Queen Elizabeth

was contented with the evasive answer of Melville, when hard pressed with the trying question, whether Queen Mary or she were the fairest. We are willing, in the spirit of that answer, to say, that the Themis of Westminster Hall is the best fitted to preside over the administration of the larger, and more fertile country of beef and pudding; while she of the te-totum (placed in that precarious position, we presume, to express her instability, since these new lights were struck out) claims a more limited but equally respectful homage, within her ancient jurisdiction—*sua paupera regna*—the Land of Cakes. If this compromise does not appease the ardour of our brethren for converting us to English forms and fashions, we must use the scriptural question, " Who hath required these things at your hands ?"

The inquiries and result of another Commission are too much to the purpose to be suppressed. The object was to investigate the conduct of the Revenue Boards in Ireland and Scotland. In the former, it is well known, great mismanagement was discovered ; for Pat, poor fellow, had been playing the loon to a considerable ex-

D

tent.   In Scotland, *not a shadow of abuse prevailed.* You would have thought, Mr Journalist, that the Irish Boards would have been re-
formed in some shape, and the Scotch establishments honourably acquitted, and suffered to continue on the footing of independence which they
had so long enjoyed, and of which they had
proved themselves so worthy.   Not so, sir.   The
Revenue Boards, in both countries, underwent
exactly the same regulation, were deprived of
their independent consequence, and placed under the superintendence of English control; the
innocent and the guilty being treated in every
respect alike.   Now, on the side of Scotland, this
was like Trinculo losing his bottle in the pool
—there was not only dishonour in the thing,
but an infinite loss.

I have heard two reasons suggested for this
indiscriminating application of punishment to
the innocent and to the culpable.

In the first place, it was honestly confessed
that Ireland would never have quietly submit-
ted to the indignity offered to her, unless poor
inoffensive Scotland had been included in the
regulation.   The Green Isle, it seems, was of

the mind of a celebrated lady of quality, who, being about to have a decayed tooth drawn, refused to submit to the operation till she had seen the dentist extract a sound and serviceable grinder from the jaws of her waiting-woman—and her humour was to be gratified. The lady was a termagant dame—the wench a tame-spirited simpleton—the dentist an obliging operator— and the teeth of both were drawn accordingly.

This gratification of his humours is gained by Pat's being up with the pike and shilelah on any or no occasion. God forbid Scotland should retrograde towards such a state—much better that the Deil, as in Burns's song, danced away with the whole excisemen in the country. We do not want to hear her prate of her number of millions of men, and her old military exploits. We had better remain in union with England, even at the risk of becoming a subordinate species of Northumberland, as far as national consequence is concerned, than remedy ourselves by even hinting the possibility of a rupture. But there is no harm in wishing Scotland to have just so much ill-nature, according to her own proverb, as may keep her good-nature from being abused ; so much national spirit as may determine her to stand by her own rights, conducting her assertion of them with every feeling of respect and amity towards England.

The other reason alleged for this equal distribution of *punishment*, as if it had been the influence of the common sun, or the general rain, to the just and the unjust, was one which is extremely predominant at present with our Ministers—the *necessity of* UNIFORMITY in all such cases; and the consideration what an awkward thing it would be to have a Board of Excise or Customs remaining independent in the one country, solely because they had, without impeachment, discharged their duty; while the same establishment was cashiered in another, for no better reason than that it had been misused.

This reminds us of an incident, said to have befallen at the Castle of Glammis, when these venerable towers were inhabited by a certain old Earl of Strathmore, who was as great an admirer of uniformity as the Chancellor of the Exchequer could have desired. He and his gardener directed all in the garden and pleasure-

grounds upon the ancient principle of exact correspondence between the different parts, so that
each alley had its brother ; a principle which,
renounced by gardeners, is now adopted by
statesmen. It chanced once upon a time that a
fellow was caught committing some petty theft,
and, being taken in the manner, was sentenced
by the Baillie MacWheeble of the jurisdiction
to stand for a certain time in the baronial pillory, called the *jougs*, being a collar and chain,
one of which contrivances was attached to each
side of the portal of the great avenue which led
to the castle. The thief was turned over accordingly to the gardener as ground-officer, to see
the punishment duly inflicted. When the Thane
of Glammis returned from his morning ride, he
was surprised to find both sides of the gate-way
accommodated each with a prisoner, like a pair of
heraldic supporters *chained* and *collared proper*.
He asked the gardener, whom he found watching
the place of punishment, as his duty required,
whether another delinquent had been detected ?
" No, my Lord," said the gardener, in the tone of
a man excellently well satisfied with himself,—
" but I thought the single fellow looked very

awkward standing on one side of the gate-way, so I gave half-a-crown to one of the labourers to stand on the other side *for uniformity's sake.*" This is exactly a case in point, and probably the only one which can be found—with this sole difference, that I do not hear that the Members of the Scottish Revenue Board got any boon for standing in the pillory with those of Ireland—for uniformity's sake.

Lastly, sir, I come to this business of extending the provisions of the Bill prohibiting the issue of notes under L.5 to Scotland, in six months after the period that the regulation shall be adopted in England.

I am not about to enter upon the question which so much agitates speculative writers upon the wealth of nations, or attempt to discuss what proportion of the precious metals ought to be detained within a country; what are the best means of keeping it there; or to what extent the want of specie can be supplied by paper credit: I will not ask if a poor man can be made a rich one, by compelling him to buy a service of plate, instead of the delf ware which served his turn. These are questions I am not adequate to solve.

But I beg leave to consider the question in a practical point of view, and to refer myself entirely to experience.

I assume, without much hazard of contradiction, that Banks have existed in Scotland for near one hundred and twenty years—that they have flourished, and the country has flourished with them—and that during the last fifty years particularly, provincial Banks, or branches of the principal established and chartered Banks, have gradually extended themselves in almost every Lowland district in Scotland; that the notes, and especially the small notes, which they distribute, entirely supply the demand for a medium of currency; and that the system has so completely expelled gold from the country of Scotland, that you never by any chance espy a guinea there, unless in the purse of an accidental stranger, or in the coffers of these Banks themselves. This is granting the facts of the case as broadly as can be asked.

It is not less unquestionable, that the consequence of this Banking system, as conducted in Scotland, has been attended with the greatest advantage to the country. The facility which it has afforded to the industrious and enterprising agriculturist or manufacturer, as well as to the trustees of the public in executing national works, has converted Scotland, from a poor, miserable, and barren country, into one, where, if Nature has done less, Art and Industry have done more, than in perhaps any country in Europe, England herself not excepted. Through means of the credit which this system has afforded, roads have been made, bridges built, and canals dug, opening up to reciprocal communication the most sequestered districts of the country—manufactures have been established, unequalled in extent or success—wastes have been converted into productive farms—the productions of the earth for human use have been multiplied twentyfold, while the wealth of the rich, and the comforts of the poor, have been extended in the same proportion. And all this in a country where the rigour of the climate, and sterility of the soil, seem united to set improvement at defiance. Let those who remember Scotland forty years since, bear witness if I speak truth or falsehood.

There is no doubt that this change has been

produced by the facilities of procuring credit, which the Scottish Banks held forth, both by discounting bills, and by granting cash-accounts. Every undertaking of consequence, whether by the public or by individuals, has been carried on by such means ; at least exceptions are extremely rare.

There is as little doubt that the Banks could not have furnished these necessary funds of cash, without enjoying the reciprocal advantage of their own notes being circulated in consequence, and by means of the accommodation thus afforded. It is not to be expected that every undertaking which the system enabled speculators or adventurers to commence, should be well-judged, attentively carried on, or successful in issue. Imprudence in some cases, misfortune in others, have had their usual quantity of victims. But in Scotland, as elsewhere, it has happened in many instances that improvements, which turned out ruinous to those who undertook them, have, notwithstanding, themselves ultimately produced the most beneficial advantages to the country, which derived in such instances an addition to its general prosperity, even from the undertakings which had proved destructive to the private fortune of the projectors.

Not only did the Banks dispersed throughout Scotland afford the means of bringing the country to an unexpected and almost marvellous degree of prosperity, but in no considerable instance, save one, have their own over-speculating undertakings been the means of interrupting that prosperity. The solitary exception was the undertaking called the Ayr Bank, rashly entered into by a large body of country gentlemen and others, unacquainted with commercial affairs, and who had moreover the misfortune not only to set out on false principles, but to get false rogues for their principal agents and managers. The fall of this Bank brought much calamity on the country ; but two things are remarkable in its history : First, that under its too prodigal, yet beneficial influence, a fine county (that of Ayr) was converted from a desert into a fertile land. 2dly, That, though at a distant interval, the Ayr Bank paid all its engagements, and the loss only fell on the original stockholders. The warning was, however, a terrible one, and has been so well attended to in Scotland, that very few attempts seem to have been afterwards made to establish Banks prematurely—that is, where the particular district was not in such an advanced state as to require the support of additional credit ; for in every such case, it was judicious-ly foreseen, the forcing a capital on the district could only lead to wild speculation, instead of supporting solid and promising undertakings.

The character and condition of the persons pursuing the profession, ought to be noticed, however slightly The Bankers of Scotland have been, generally speaking, *good* men, in the mercantile phrase, showing, by the wealth of which they have died possessed, that their cre-dit was sound ; and *good* men also, many of them eminently so, in the more extensive and better sense of the word, manifesting, by the excellence of their character, the fairness of the means by which their riches were acquired. There may have been, among so numerous a body, men of a different character, fishers in troubled waters, capitalists who sought gain not by the encouragement of fair trade and ho-nest industry, but by affording temporary fuel to rashness or avarice. But the number of up-right traders in the profession has narrowed the

means of mischief, which such Christian Shy-
locks would otherwise have possessed. There
was loss, there was discredit, in having recourse
to such characters, when honest wants could be
fairly supplied by upright men, and on liberal
terms. Such reptiles have been confined in Scotland to batten upon their proper prey of folly,
and feast, like worms, on the corruption in which
they are bred.

Since the period of the Ayr Bank, now near
half a century, I recollect very few instances
of Banking Companies issuing notes, which have
become insolvent. One, about thirty years
since, was the Merchant Bank of Stirling, which
never was in high credit, having been known
almost at the time of its commencement by the
ominous nick-name of *Black in the West*. Another was within these ten years, the East-
Lothian Banking Company, whose affairs had
been very ill conducted by a villainous manager.
In both cases, the notes were paid up in full. In
the latter case, they were taken up by one of
the most respectable houses in Edinburgh;
so that all the current engagements were paid
without the least check to the circulation of
their notes, or inconvenience to poor or rich,

who happened to have them in possession. The Union Bank of Falkirk also became insolvent within these fifteen years, but paid up its engagements without much loss to the creditors. Other cases there may have occurred not coming within my recollection; but I think none which made any great sensation, or could at all affect the general confidence of the country in the stability of the system. None of these bankruptcies excited much attention, or, as we have seen, caused any considerable loss.

In the present unhappy commercial distress, I have always heard and understood, that the Scottish Banks have done all in their power to alleviate the evils which came thickening on the country; and far from acting illiberally, that they have come forward to support the tottering credit of the commercial world with a frankness which augured the most perfect confidence in their own resources. We have heard of only one provincial Bank being even for a moment in the predicament of suspicion; and of that copartnery the funds and credit were so well understood, that their correspondents in Edinburgh, as in the case of the East Lothian Bank formerly mentioned, at once guaranteed the payment of their notes, and saved the public even from momentary agitation, and individuals from the possibility of distress. I ask what must be the stability of a system of credit, of which such an universal earthquake could not displace or shake even the slightest individual portion?

Thus stands the case in Scotland; and it is clear, any restrictive enactment affecting the Banking system, or their mode of issuing notes, must be adopted in consequence of evils, operating elsewhere perhaps, but certainly unknown in this country.

In England, unfortunately, things have been very different, and the insolvency of many provincial Banking Companies, of the most established reputation for stability, has greatly distressed the country, and alarmed London itself, from the necessary re-action of their misfortunes upon their correspondents in the capital.

I do not think, sir, that the advocate of Scotland is called upon to go farther, in order to plead an exemption from any experiment which England may think proper to try to cure her own malady, than to say such malady does not exist in her jurisdiction. It is surely enough to plead, " We are well, our pulse and complexion

prove it—let those who are sick take physic."
But the opinion of the English Ministers is
widely different; for, granting our premises,
they deny our conclusion.

The peculiar humour of a friend, whom I lost
some years ago, is the only one I recollect, which
jumps precisely with the reasoning of the Chancellor of the Exchequer. My friend was an old
Scottish laird, a bachelor and a humourist—
wealthy, convivial, and hospitable, and of course
having always plenty of company about him.
He had a regular custom of swallowing every
night in the world one of Dr Anderson's pills,
for which reasons may be readily imagined.
But it is not so easy to account for his insisting
on every one of his guests taking the same medicine; and whether it was by way of patroni
zing the medicine, which is in some sense a
national receipt, or whether the mischievous
old wag amused himself with anticipating the
scenes of delicate embarrassment, which the dis-
pensation sometimes produced in the course of
the night, I really cannot even guess. What
is equally strange, he pressed this request with
a sort of eloquence, which succeeded with every
guest. No man escaped, though there were few

who did not make resistance. His powers of persuasion would have been invaluable to a minister of state. "What! not one *Leetle Anderson*, to oblige your friend, your host, your entertainer! He had taken one himself—he would take another, if you pleased—Surely what was good for his complaints must of course be beneficial to yours?" It was in vain you pleaded your being perfectly well,—your detesting the medicine, —your being certain it would not agree with you —none of the apologies were received as valid. You might be warm, pathetic or sulky, fretful or patient, grave or serious in testifying your repugnance, but you were equally a doomed man; escape was impossible. Your host was in his turn eloquent,—authoritative,—facetious,—argumentative,—precatory,—pathetic, above all, pertinacious. No guest was known to escape the *Leetle Anderson*. The last time I experienced the laird's hospitality, there were present at the evening meal the following catalogue of guests: A Bond-street Dandy, of the most brilliant water, drawn thither by the temptation of grouse-shooting—a writer from the neighbouring borough, (the laird's *Doer*, I believe,)—two coun-

try lairds, men of reserved and stiff habits—
three sheep-farmers, as stiff-necked and stubborn
as their own halter'd rams—and I, Malachi Malagrowther, not facile or obvious to persuasion.
There was also the Esculapius of the vicinity—
one who gave, but elsewhere was never known
to *take* medicine. All succumbed—each took, after
various degrees of resistance according to his
peculiar fashion, his own *Leetle Anderson.* The
Doer took a brace. On the event I am silent.
None had reason to congratulate himself on his
complaisance. The laird has slept with his ancestors for some years, remembered sometimes
with a smile on account of his humorous eccen-
tricities, always with a sigh when his surviving
friends and neighbours reflect on his kindliness
and genuine beneficence. I have only to add,
that I hope he has not bequeathed to the Chancellor of the Exchequer, otherwise so highly
gifted, his invincible powers of persuading folks
to take medicine, which their constitutions do
not require.

Have I argued my case too high in supposing
that the present intended legislative enactment
is as inapplicable to Scotland, as a pair of elabo-

E

rate knee-buckles would be to the dress of a kilted Highlander? I think not.

I understand Lord Liverpool and the Chancellor of the Exchequer distinctly to have admitted the fact, that no distress whatever had originated in Scotland from the present issuing of small notes of the Bankers established there, whether provincial in the strict sense, or sent abroad by branches of the larger establishments settled in the metropolis. No proof can be desired better than the admission of the adversary.

Nevertheless, we have been positively informed by the newspapers that Ministers see no reason why any law adopted on this subject should not be imperative over all his Majesty's dominions, including Scotland, *for uniformity's sake*. In my opinion, they might as well make a law that the Scotsman, for uniformity's sake, should not eat oatmeal, because it is found to give Englishmen the heart-burn. If an ordinance prohibiting the oat-cake, can be accompanied with a regulation capable of being enforced, that in future, for uniformity's sake, our moors and uplands shall henceforth bear the purest wheat, I for one have no objection to the regulation. But till Ben-Nevis be level with Norfolkshire, though the natural wants of the two nations may be the same, the extent of these wants, natural or commercial, and the mode of supplying them, must be widely different, let the rule of uniformity be as absolute as it will. The nation which cannot raise wheat, must be allowed to eat oat-bread; the nation which is too poor to retain a circulating medium of the precious metals, must be permitted to supply its place with paper credit; otherwise, they must go without food, and without currency.

If I were called on, Mr Journalist, I think I could give some reasons why the system of Banking which has been found well adapted for Scotland is not proper for England, and why there is no reason for inflicting upon us the intended remedy; in other words, why this political balsam of Fierabras, which is to relieve Don Quixote, may have a great chance to poison Sancho. With this view, I will mention briefly some strong points of distinction affecting the comparative credit of the Banks in England and in Scotland ; and they seem such as to furnish, to one inexperienced in political economics, (upon the transcendental doctrines of which so much stress is now laid,) very satisfactory reasons for the difference which is not denied to exist betwixt the effects of the same general system in different countries.

In Scotland, almost all Banking Companies consist of a considerable number of persons, many of them men of landed property, whose landed estates, with the burthens legally affecting them, may be learned from the records, for the expense of a few shillings ; so that all the world knows, or may know, the general basis on which their credit rests, and the extent of real property, which, independent of their personal means, is responsible for their commercial engagements. In most Banking Establishments this fund of credit is considerable, in others immense ; especially in those where the shares are numerous, and are held in small proportions, many of them by persons of landed estates, whose fortunes, however large, and however small their share of stock, must be all liable to the engagements of the Bank. In England, as I believe, the number of the partners engaged in a Banking concern cannot exceed five ; and though of late years their landed property has been declared subject to be attached by their commercial creditors, yet no one can learn, without incalculable trouble, the real value of that land, or with what mortgages it is burthened. Thus, *cæteris paribus,* the English Banker cannot make his solvency manifest to the public, therefore cannot expect, or receive, the same unlimited trust, which is willingly and securely reposed in those of the same profession in Scotland.

Secondly, the circulation of the Scottish bank-notes is free and unlimited ; an advantage arising from their superior degree of credit. They pass without a shadow of objection through the whole limits of Scotland, and, although they cannot be legally tendered, are current nearly as far as York, in England. Those of English Banking Companies seldom extend beyond a very limited horizon : in two or three stages from the place where they are issued, many of them are objected to, and give perpetual trouble to any traveller who has happened to take them in change on the road. Even the most creditable provincial notes never approach London in a free tide—never circulate like blood to the heart, and from thence to the extremities, but are current within a limited circle ; often, indeed, so very limited, that the notes issued in the morning, to use an old simile, fly out like pigeons from the dovecot, and are sure to return in the evening to the spot which they have left at break of day.

Owing to these causes, and others which I forbear mentioning, the profession of provincial Bankers in England is limited in its regular profits, and uncertain in its returns, to a degree unknown in Scotland ; and is, therefore, more apt to be adopted in the south by men of sanguine hopes and bold adventure, (both frequently disproportioned to the extent of their capital,) who sink in mines, or other hazardous speculations, the funds which their banking credit enables them to command, and deluge the country with notes, which, on some unhappy morning, are found not worth a penny ;—as those to whom the foul fiend has given apparent treasures, are said in due time to discover they are only pieces of slate.

I am aware it may be urged, that the restrictions imposed on those English provincial Banks are necessary to secure the supremacy of the Bank of England; on the same principle on which dogs kept near the purlieus of a royal forest, were anciently lamed by the cutting off of one of the claws, to prevent their interfering with the royal sport. This is a very good regulation for England, for what I know; but why should the Scottish institutions, which do not, and cannot, interfere with the influence of the Bank of England, be put on a level with those of which such jealousy is, justly or unjustly, entertained? We receive no benefit from that immense Establishment, which, like a great oak, overshadows England from Tweed to Cornwall—Why should our national plantations be cut down or cramped for the sake of what affords us neither shade nor shelter, and which besides can take no advantage by the injury done to us? Why should we be subjected to a monopoly, from which we derive no national benefit?

I have only to add, that Scotland has not felt the slightest inconvenience from the want of specie, nay, that it has never been in request among

them. A tradesman will take a guinea more unwillingly than a note of the same value—to the
peasant the coin is unknown. No one ever wishes
for specie save when upon a journey to England. In occasional runs upon particular houses,
the notes of other Banking Companies have always been the value asked for—no holder of
these notes ever demanded specie. The credit
of one establishment might be doubted for the
time—that of the general system was never
brought into question. Even Avarice, the most
suspicious of passions, has in no instance I ever
heard of, desired to compose her hoards by an
accumulation of the precious metals. The confidence in the credit of our ordinary medium
has not been doubted even in the dreams of the
most irritable and jealous of human passions.

All these considerations are so obvious, that a
statesman so acute as Mr Robinson must have
taken them in at the first glance, and must at the
same time have deemed them of no weight, compared with the necessary conformity between the
laws of the two kingdoms. I must, therefore,
speak to the justice of this point of uniformity.

Sir, my respected ancestor, Sir Mungo, when

he had the distinguished honour to be *whipping*, or rather *whipped boy*, to his Majesty James the Sixth of gracious memory, was always, in virtue of his office, scourged when the King deserved flogging ; and the same equitable rule seems to distinguish the conduct of Government towards Scotland, as one of the three United Kingdoms.   If Pat is guilty of peculation, Sister Peg loses her Boards of Revenue— if John Bull's cashiers mismanage his money-matters, those who have conducted Sister Margaret's to their own great honour, and her no less advantage, must be deprived of the power of serving her in future ; at least that power must be greatly restricted and limited.

" Quidquid delirant reges plectuntur Achivi."

That is to say, if our superiors of England and Ireland eat sour grapes, the Scottish teeth must be set on edge as well as their own.   An uniformity in benefits may be well—an uniformity in penal measures, towards the innocent and the guilty, in prohibitory regulations, whether necessary or not, seems harsh law, and worse justice.

This levelling system, not equitable in itself, is infinitely unjust, if a story, often told by my poor old grandfather, was true, which I own I am inclined to doubt. The old man, sir, had learned in his youth, or dreamed in his dotage, that Scotland had become an integral part of England,—not in right of conquest, or rendition, or through any right of inheritance,—but in virtue of a solemn Treaty of Union. Nay, so distinct an idea had he of this supposed Treaty, that he used to recite one of its articles to this effect :—" That the laws in use within the kingdom of Scotland, do, after the Union, remain in the same force as before, but alterable by the Parliament of Great Britain, with this difference between the laws concerning public right, policy, and civil government, and those which concern private right, that the former may be made the same through the whole United Kingdom ; but that no alteration be made on laws which concern private right, *excepting for the evident utility of the subjects within Scotland.*" When the old gentleman came to the passage, which you will mark in italics, he always clenched his fist, and exclaimed, " *Nemo me impune*

lacesset !" which, I presume, are words belonging to the black art, since there is no one in the
Modern Athens conjuror enough to understand
their meaning, or at least to comprehend the
spirit of the sentiment which my grandfather
thought they conveyed.

I cannot help thinking, sir, that if there had
been any truth in my grandfather's story, some
Scottish Member would, on the late occasion,
have informed the Chancellor of the Exchequer,
that, in virtue of this Treaty, it was no sufficient reason for innovating upon the private
rights of Scotsmen in a most tender and delicate point, merely that the Right Honourable
Gentleman saw no reason why the same law
should not be current through the whole of his
Majesty's dominions ; and that, on the contrary,
it was incumbent upon him to go a step further,
and to show that the alteration proposed *was*
for the EVIDENT UTILITY *of the subjects within
Scotland,*—a proposition disavowed by the Right
Honourable Gentleman's candid admission, as
well as by that of the Prime Minister, and con-
tradicted in every circumstance by the actual
state of the case.

Methinks, sir, our " Chosen Five-and-Forty,"
supposing they had bound themselves to Ministers by such oaths of silence and obedience, as
are taken by Carthusian friars, must have had
free-will and speech to express their sentiments,
had they been possessed of so irrefragable an
argument in such a case of extremity. The sight
of a father's life in danger is said to have restored the power of language to the dumb ; and
truly, the necessary defence of the rights of our
native country is not, or at least ought not to
be, a less animating motive. Lord Lauderdale
almost alone interfered, and procured, to his infinite honour, a delay of six months in the extension of this act,—a sort of reprieve from the
southern *jougs*,—by which we may have some
chance of profiting, if, during the interval, we
can show ourselves true Scotsmen, by some better proof than merely by being " wise behind
the hand."

In the first place, sir, I would have this Old
Treaty searched for, and should it be found to
be still existing, I think it decides the question.
For, how can it be possible, that it should be
for the " evident utility" of Scotland to alter

her laws of private right, to the total subversion of a system under which she is admitted to have flourished for a century, and which has never within North Britain been attended with the inconveniencies charged against it in the sister country, where, by the way, it never existed? Even if the old parchment should be voted obsolete, there would be some satisfaction in having it looked out and preserved—not in the Register-Office, or Advocates' Library, where it might awaken painful recollections—but in the Museum of the Antiquaries, where, with the Solemn League and Covenant, the Letter of the Scottish Nobles to the Pope on the independence of their country, and other antiquated documents once held in reverence, it might silently contract dust, yet remain to bear witness that such things had been.

I earnestly hope, however, that an international league of such importance may still be found obligatory on both the *high* and the *low* contracting parties; on that which has the power, and apparently the will, to break it, as well as on the weaker nation, who cannot, without incurring still worse, and more miserable consequences, oppose aggression, otherwise than by invoking the faith of treaties, and the national honour of Old England.

In the second place, all ranks and bodies of men in North Britain, (for all are concerned, the poor as well as the rich,) should express by petition their sense of the injustice which is offered to the country, and the distress which will probably be the necessary consequence. Without the power of issuing their own notes, the Banks cannot supply the manufacturer with that credit which enables him to pay his workmen, and wait his return ; or accommodate the farmer with that fund which makes it easy for him to discharge his rent, and give wages to his labourers, while in the act of performing expensive operations which are to treble or quadruple the produce of his farm. The trustees on the high-roads and other public works, so ready to stake their personal credit for carrying on public improvements, will no longer possess the power of raising funds by doing so. The whole existing state of credit is to be altered from top to bottom, and Ministers are silent on any remedy which such a state of things would imperiously require.

These are subjects worth struggling for, and rather of more importance than generally come before County Meetings. The English legislature seems inclined to stultify our Law Authorities in their department; but let us at least try if they will listen to the united voice of a Nation in matters which so intimately concern its welfare, that almost every man must have formed a judgment on the subject, from something like personal experience. For my part, I cannot doubt the result.

Times are undoubtedly different from those of Queen Anne, when, Dean Swift having in a political pamphlet passed some sarcasms on the Scottish nation, as a poor and fierce people, the Scythians of Britain,—the Scottish Peers, headed by the Duke of Argyle, went in a body to the Ministers, and compelled them to disown the sentiments which had been expressed by their partizan, and offer a reward of L.300 for the author of the libel, well known to be the best advocate and most intimate frined of the existing administration. They demanded also, that the printer and publisher should be prosecuted before the House of Peers; and Harley, however unwillingly, was obliged to yield to their demand

In the celebrated case of Porteous, the English legislature saw themselves compelled to desist from vindictive measures, on account of a gross offence committed in the Metropolis of Scotland. In that of the Roman Catholic bill, they yielded to the voice of the Scottish people, or rather of the Scottish mob, and declared the proposed alteration of the Law should not extend to North Britain. The cases were different, in point of merit, though the Scots were successful in both. In the one, a boon of clemency was extorted ; in the other, concession was an act of decided weakness. But ought the present administration of Great Britain to show less deference to our temperate and general remonstrance, on a matter concerning ourselves only, than their predecessors did to the passions, and even the ill-founded and unjust prejudices, of our ancestors ?

Times, indeed, have changed since those days, and circumstances also. We are no longer a poor, that is, so *very poor* a country and people ; and as we have increased in wealth, we have become somewhat poorer in spirit, and more loath to incur displeasure by contests upon mere etiquette, or national prejudice. But we have some grounds to plead for favour with England. We have borne our pecuniary impositions, during a long war, with a patience the more exemplary, as they lay heavier on us from our comparative want of means—our blood has flowed as freely as that of England or of Ireland—our lives and fortunes have been as unhesitatingly devoted to the defence of the empire—our loyalty as warmly and willingly displayed towards the person of our Sovereign. We have consented with submission, if not with cheerfulness, to reductions and abolitions of public offices, required for the good of the state at large, but which must affect materially the condition, and even the respectability, of our over-burthened aristocracy. We have in every respect conducted ourselves as good and faithful subjects of the general Empire.

We do not boast of these things as actual merits ; but they are at least duties discharged, and in an appeal to men of honour and of judgment, must entitle us to be heard with patience, and even deference, on the management of our own affairs, if we speak unanimously, lay aside party feeling, and use the voice of one leaf of the holy

F

Trefoil,—one distinct and component part of the United Kingdoms.

Let no consideration deter us from pleading our own cause temperately but firmly, and we shall certainly receive a favourable audience. Even our acquisition of a little wealth, which might abate our courage on other occasions, should invigorate us to unanimous persever- ance at the present crisis, when the very source of our national prosperity is directly, though unwittingly, struck at. Our plaids are, I trust, not yet sunk into Jewish gaberdines, to be wan- tonly spit upon ; nor are we yet bound to " re- ceive the insult with a patient shrug." But ex- ertion is now demanded on other accounts than those of mere honourable punctilio. Misers themselves will struggle in defence of their property, though tolerant of all aggressions by which that is not threatened. Avarice herself, however mean-spirited, will rouse to defend the wealth she possesses, and preserve the means of gaining more. Scotland is now called upon to rally in defence of the sources of her national im- provement, and the means of increasing it ; upon which, as none are so much concerned in the subject, none can be such competent judges as Scotsmen themselves.

I cannot believe so generous a people as the English, so wise an administration as the present, will disregard our humble remonstrances, merely because they are made in the form of peaceful entreaty, and not *secundum perfervidum ingenium Scotorum*, with " durk and pistol at our belt." It would be a dangerous lesson to teach the empire at large, that threats can extort what is not yielded to reasonable and respectful remonstrance.

But this is not all. The principle of " uniformity of laws," if not manfully withstood, may have other blessings in store for us. Suppose, that when finished with blistering Scotland while she is in perfect health, England should find time and courage to withdraw the veil from the deep cancer which is gnawing her own bowels, and make an attempt to stop the fatal progress of her *poor-rates*. Some system or other must be proposed in its place—a grinding one it must be, for it is not an evil to be cured by palliatives. Suppose the English, for uniformity's sake, insist

that Scotland, which is at present free from this
foul and shameful disorder, should nevertheless
be included in the severe *treatment* which the
disease demands, how would the landholders of
Scotland like to undergo the scalpel and cautery,
merely because England requires to be scari-
fied ?

Or again ;—Supposing England should take
a fancy to impart to us her sanguinary criminal
code, which, too cruel to be carried into effect,
gives every wretch that is condemned a chance
of one to twelve that he shall not be executed,
and so turns the law into a lottery—would this
be an agreeable boon to North Britain ?

Once more ;—What if the English ministers
should feel disposed to extend to us their equitable system of process respecting civil debt,
which divides the advantages so admirably betwixt debtor and creditor—*That* equal dispen-
sation of justice, which provides that an im-
prisoned debtor, if a rogue, may remain in undisturbed possession of a great landed estate, and
enjoy in a jail all the luxuries of Sardanapalus,
while the wretch to whom he owes money is starving : and that, to balance the matter, a creditor,

if cruel, may detain a debtor in prison for a life-
time, and make, as the established phrase goes,
dice of his bones—Would this admirable recipro-
city of privilege, indulged alternately to knave
and tyrant, please Saunders better than his own
humane action of Cessio, and his equitable process of Adjudication ?

I will not insist farther on such topics, for I
dare say, that these apparent enormities in principle are, in England where they have operation,
modified and corrected in practice by circumstances unknown to me ; so that in passing judgement on them, I may myself fall into the error I
deprecate, of judging of foreign laws without being aware of all the premises. Neither do I mean
that we should struggle with illiberality against
any improvements which can be borrowed from
English principle. I would only desire that
such ameliorations were adopted, not merely
because they are English, but because they are
suited to be assimilated with the laws of Scotland, and lead, in short, *to her evident utility;*
and this on the principle, that in transplanting
a tree, little attention need be paid to the character of the climate and soil from which it is

brought, although the greatest care must be
taken that those of the situation to which it is
transplanted are fitted to receive it. It would
be no reason for planting mulberry-trees in
Scotland, that they luxuriate in the south of
England. There is sense in the old proverb,
" Ilk land has its ain lauch."

In the present case, it is impossible to believe
the extension of these restrictions to Scotland can
be for the *evident utility* of the country, which
has prospered so long and so uniformly under
directly the contrary system.

It is very probable I may be deemed illiberal
in all this reasoning ; but if to look for information to practical results, rather than to theoretical principles, and to argue from the effect
of the experience of a century, rather than the
deductions of a modern hypothesis, be illiberality, I must sit down content with a censure,
which will include wiser men than I. The philosophical tailors of Laputa, who wrought by
mathematical calculation, had, no doubt, a supreme contempt for those humble fashioners who
went to work by measuring the person of their
customer ; but Gulliver tells us, that the worst

clothes he ever wore, were constructed upon abstract principles; and truly I think we have seen some laws, and may see more, not much better adapted to existing circumstances, than the Captain's philosophical uniform to his actual person.

It is true, that every wise statesman keeps sound and general political principles in his eye, as the pilot looks upon his compass to discover his true course. But this true course cannot always be followed out straight and diametrically; it must be altered from time to time, nay, sometimes apparently abandoned, on account of shoals, breakers, and headlands, not to mention contrary winds. The same obstacles occur to the course of the Statesman. The point at which he aims may be important, the principle on which he steers may be just; yet the obstacles arising from rooted prejudices, from intemperate passions, from ancient practices, from a different character of people, from varieties in climate and soil, may cause a direct movement upon his ultimate object to be attended with distress to individuals, and loss to the community, which no good man would wish to occasion, and with dangers which no wise man would voluntarily choose to encounter.

Although I think the Chancellor of the Exchequer has been rather precipitate in the decided opinion which he is represented to have expressed on this occasion, I am far from entertaining the slightest disrespect for the right honourable Gentleman. " I hear as good exclamation upon him as on any man in Messina, and though I am but a poor man, I am glad to hear it." But a decided attachment to abstract principle, and to a spirit of generalizing, is—like a rash rider on a headstrong horse—very apt to run foul of local obstacles, which might have been avoided by a more deliberate career, where the nature of the ground had been previously considered.

I make allowance for the temptation natural to an ingenious and active mind. There is a natural pride in following out an universal and levelling principle. It seems to augur genius, force of conception, and steadiness of purpose ; qualities which every legislator is desirous of being thought to possess. On the other hand, the study of local advantages and impediments demands labour and inquiry, and is rewarded after all only with the cold and parsimonious praise due to humble industry. It is no less true, however, that measures which go straight and direct to a great general object, without noticing intervening impediments, must often resemble the fierce progress of the thunderbolt or the canon-ball, those dreadful agents, which, in rushing right to their point, care not what ruin they make by the way. The sounder and more moderate policy, accommodating its measures to exterior circumstances, rather resembles the judicious course of a well-conducted highway, which, turning aside frequently from its direct course,

" Winds round the corn-field and the hill of vines,"

and becomes devious, that it may respect property and avoid obstacles ; thus escaping even temporary evils, and serving the public no less in its more circuitous, than it would have done in its direct course.

Can you tell me, sir, if this *uniformity* of civil institutions, which calls for such sacrifices, be at all descended from, or related to, a doctrine nearly of the same name, called Conformity in religious doctrine, very fashionable about 150 years since, which undertook to unite the jarring creeds of the United Kingdom to one common standard, and excited a universal strife by the vain attempt, and a thousand fierce disputes, in which she

> " ————— umpire sate,
> And by decision more embroil'd the fray ?"

Should Uniformity have the same pedigree, Malachi Malagrowther proclaims her " a hawk of a very bad nest."

The universal opinion of a whole kingdom, founded upon a century's experience, ought not to be lightly considered as founded in ignorance and prejudice. I am something of an agriculturist; and in travelling through the country, I have often had occasion to wonder that the inhabitants of particular districts had not adopted certain obvious improvements in cultivation. But, upon inquiry, I have usually found that appearances had deceived me, and that I had not reckoned on particular local circumstances, which either prevented the execution of the system I should have theoretically recommended, or rendered some other more advantageous in the particular circumstances.

I do not therefore resist theoretical innovation in general ; I only humbly desire it may not outrun the suggestions arising from the experience of ages. I would have the necessity felt and acknowledged before old institutions are demolished—the *evident utility* of every alteration demonstrated before it is adopted upon mere speculation. I submit our ancient system to the pruning-knife of the legislature, but would not willingly see our reformers employ a weapon, which, like the sword of Jack the Giant-Killer, *cuts before the point.*

It is always to be considered, that in human affairs, the very best imaginable result is seldom to be obtained, and that it is wise to content ourselves with the best which can be got. This principle speaks with a voice of thunder against violent innovation, for the sake of possible improvement, where things are already well. We ought not to desire better bread than is made of wheat. Our Scottish proverb warns us to *let weel bide;* and all the world has heard of the untranslateable Italian epitaph upon the man, who died of taking physic to make him better, when he was already in health.

I am, Mr Journalist,

Yours,

MALACHI MALAGROWTHER.

POSTSCRIPT.

Since writing these hasty thoughts, I hear it reported that we are to have an extension of our precarious reprieve, and that our six months are to be extended to six years. I would not have Scotland trust to this hollow truce. The measure ought, like all others, to be canvassed on its merits, and frankly admitted or rejected; it has been stirred, and ought to be decided. I request my countrymen not to be soothed into inactivity by that temporizing, and, I will say, unmanly vacillation. Government is pledged to nothing

by taking an open course ; for if the bill, so far
as applicable to Scotland, is at present absolutely laid aside, there can be no objection to their
resuming it at any period, when, from change
of circumstances, it may be advantageous to
Scotland, and when, for what I know, it may
be welcomed as a boon.

But if held over our heads as a minatory
measure, to take place within a certain period,
what can the event be but to cripple and ultimately destroy the present system, on which a
direct attack is found at present inexpedient ?
Can the Bankers continue to conduct their profession on the same secure footing, with an abro-
gation of it in prospect ? Must it not cease to
be what it has hitherto been—a business carried on both for their own profit, and for the accommodation of the country ? Instead of em-
ploying their capital in the usual channels, must
they not in self-defence employ it in forming
others ? Will not the substantial and wealthy
withdraw their funds from that species of commerce ? And may not the place of these be
supplied by men of daring adventure, without

corresponding capital, who will take a chance of wealth or ruin in the chances of the game?

If it is the absolute and irrevocable determination that the bill is to be extended to us, the sooner the great penalty is inflicted the better; for in politics and commerce, as in all the other affairs of life, absolute and certain evil is better than uncertainty and protracted suspense.

EDINBURGH:
PRINTED BY JAMES BALLANTYNE AND CO.

A

SECOND LETTER

TO THE

Editor of the Edinburgh Weekly Journal,

FROM

MALACHI MALAGROWTHER, Esq.

ON THE

PROPOSED CHANGE OF CURRENCY,

AND

OTHER LATE ALTERATIONS,

AS THEY AFFECT, OR ARE INTENDED TO AFFECT,

THE

KINGDOM OF SCOTLAND.

THIRD EDITION.

━━━━

EDINBURGH:

Printed by James Ballantyne and Company,

FOR WILLIAM BLACKWOOD, EDINBURGH: AND
T. CADELL, STRAND, LONDON.

━━━━

1826.

LETTER SECOND,

PROPOSED CHANGE OF CURRENCY.

———

TO THE EDITOR
OF THE EDINBURGH WEEKLY JOURNAL.

DEAR MR JOURNALIST,

WHEN I last wrote to you, I own it was with the feelings of one who discharges a painful duty, merely because he feels it to be one, and without much hope of his endeavour being useful. Swift says that kingdoms may be subject to poverty and lowness of heart as well as individuals; and that in such moments they become reckless of their own interests, and contract habits of submission, which encourage those who wish to take advantage of them to prefer the most unreason-

G

able pretensions. It was when Esau came from the harvest, faint and at point to die, that Jacob proposed to him his exorbitant bargain of the mess of pottage. There is a deep and typical mystery under the scriptural transaction ; but, taken as a simple fact, the sottish facility of the circumvented heir rather aggravates the unfeeling selfishness of the artful brother, to whom he was made a dupe. The " whoreson Apoplexy" of Scotland may be rather a case of repletion than exhaustion, but it has the same dispiriting effects.

Yet, into whatsoever deep and passive slumber our native country may have been lulled from habits of peaceful acquiescence, the Government have now found a way to awaken her. The knife has gone to the very quick, and the comatose patient is roused to most acute possession of his feelings and his intellect. The heather is on fire far and wide ; and every man, woman, and child in the country, are bound by the duty they owe to their native land, to spread the alarm and increase the blaze.

——— Jam proximus ardet
Ucalegon———

The city of Edinburgh has uttered a voice becoming the ancient Queen of the North. The Law Bodies, and the Gentry of Mid-Lothian, have set the example of petitioning Government, and proclaiming their sense of the measure designed; it has been followed in other counties, and I trust to see it soon spread into the smallest burghs, into the most wild districts of Scotland. There are none which the impending misery will not reach—there are no Scotchmen so humble that they have not a share in a national insult, so lowly that they will not suffer from a national wrong—none that are uninterested in maintaining our rights both individually, and as a people—and none, I trust, that have not spirit to do so, by all legal and peaceable means.

I congratulate you, sir, on the awakened spirit of our representatives in the two Houses of Parliament. Our true-hearted Duke of Athole, and Lord Lauderdale, whose acuteness and powers of thinking and reasoning may, without disparagement, be compared with those of any statesman now living, have set an example not to be forgotten; and we know that the slender proportion of aristocracy, which Scotland was left in possession of at the Union, entertain the same patriotic sentiments. We are equally assured of the faith of our representatives in the Lower House, and they on their part may believe they will not serve an ungrateful public. Scotland expects from them the exertions corresponding to their high trust—a trust of which they must render an account to their constituents, and that very shortly. Let every body of electors, from Dumfries to Dingwall, instruct its representative upon their own sentiments, and upon the conduct which they desire he should hold during this great national crisis; and let the Administration be aware, that if any of our Members should desert the public cause on this occasion, they are not like to have the benefit of their implicit homage in the next Parliament. Burns's address to them in jest, is language which may now be held to the Scottish representatives in serious earnest :—

> Does ony great man glunch and gloom,
> Speak out and never fash your thumb ;
> Let posts and pensions sink or soom
> Wi' those wha grant them ;
> If honestly they cannot come,
> Far better want them.

I have been told by some cautious friends, that the time for such remonstrances as I do most earnestly recommend to our Scottish representatives, would be now more unfavourable than formerly—so unfavourable, that they represent the case as desperate. Admitting all I had said in my first Epistle, these *douce* men see no resource but in the most submissive acquiescence to the commands of those in whose breasts, they say, is now lodged the uncontrolled power to listen to reason, justice, nay, compassion, or to prefer the exercise of their own pleasure to the dictates of them all. Your birthright, proceed these Job's comforters, will be taken from you at all events by superior numbers. Yield it up, therefore, with a good grace, and thank God if they give you a mess of pottage in return—it will be just so much gain. These desponding persons explain the state of total insignificance into which, they say, we have fallen, by a reference to the Irish Union, which has added an hundred more Members to Parliament; so that the handful assigned to Scotland, (which never possessed a very influential power in the House, so far as numbers go,) must

now altogether lose consideration, in opposition
to the majorities of a peremptory Minister, who,
like the " merciless Macdonald,"

from the *Western Isle,*
With Kernes and Gallow-glasses is supplied.

It requires but little arithmetic to compute,
that the fated number, forty-five, bears a less
proportion to six hundred and thirteen than to
five hundred and thirteen, the number of the
House of Commons at the time of the Scottish
Union.   Yet, sir, I am not altogether discouraged with this comfortless prospect.   I think I
can see means of relief arising even out of the
very difficulties of the case.   Let us regard the
matter somewhat more closely.

In the first place, I will consider what we can
do by our present Scottish representation,—our
own proper force.   Next, I will have a friendly
word or two with those same auxiliaries of
Ireland, whom, perhaps, the Sassenagh may
find less implicit followers in the present case,
than my chicken-hearted advisers apprehend.
Lastly, I will address myself to the English
Members, and especially to such who, on great

occasions, prefer the exercise of their own understanding to an absolute and obsequious deference to the dictates of an Administration, however much they may respect the statesmen of
whom it is composed, or are disposed to acquiesce
in the general principles on which they act.

Upon the first point I beg to remind you, that
much greater effect is derived from the decided,
conjoined, and simultaneous exertion of a comparatively small force, than from the efforts of a
more numerous body, not bound together by the
same strong ties of duty and necessity. Battles
have been often gained, and political measures
have been as frequently carried, by the determined urgency, or no less determined resistance,
of a comparatively insignificant number.

Nos numerus sumus, is a logical argument
perfectly understood by an English Minister,
and has had great weight in the scale. I will
give a ludicrous instance of this. There was of
old a certain Nobleman, who, by means of certain boroughs, sent certain members to Westminster, which members, being there, were certain to hold the same opinions with the Noble
Lord, and to vote in the House of Commons

exactly to the same tune as his Lordship in the House of Peers. The Great Man, who was the animating soul of this Holy Alliance, had occasion to ask some favour of Government. It was probably something very unreasonable—at any rate, it was so disagreeable to the Minister, that, I am told, he would as soon have relished the proposal of giving silver for a twenty-shilling note of the Bank of Scotland. The Minister made civil excuses—the Peer observed in reply—*We are seven votes.*—The Minister stopped, cleared his throat, changed his argument.—*We are seven voices*, was again the only answer.—The Great Man, usually flattered, became flatterer in his turn—he conjured—he even threatened.—The Peer was as unassailable, in his numerical proposition, by entreaty or argument, as the sweet little rustic girl in a poem which it is almost sin to parody—

> Whate'er the Minister could say,
> The Noble Lord would have his way,
> And said, *Nay, we are seven.*

They parted on these terms. The Minister retired to rest, and dreamed that he saw the pertinacious Peer advancing to storm the cabinet, after having, like the great magician Kehama, broke himself up into seven sub-divisions of equal strength, and by means of this extraordinary process of multiplication, advancing to his daring enterprise by seven avenues at once. The vision was too horrible—and a " private and confidential" note gave the necessary assurance to the Noble Lord, that the magical number Seven had as much weight in Saint Stephen's, as Dr Slop assigns to it in the Catholic mysteries ; so the seven planets continued to move regularly in their political orbit.

This is a strong proof, sir, of the *vis unita fortior*, and contains a good lesson for our Representatives upon the present occasion. It would be strange indeed, if they, to whom their country has given her confidence, should hesitate to save her from dishonour and deep distress, which may approach nigh to ruin, [I will make my words good before I have done,] when it is only necessary that they should be as determined and inflexible, where the safety of an ancient kingdom is concerned, as the selfish old borough-jobber and his political friends showed themselves pertinacious, in pursuit of some wretched personal object of private advantage.

The Scottish Members of Parliament should therefore lose no time—not an instant—in uniting together in their national character of the Representatives of Scotland. If the scene were to be the British Coffee-House, the hour half past six o'clock P.M., and the preliminaries of business a few glasses of claret to national toasts, I should not have the worse opinion of the sense of the meeting. Their first resolution should be, to lay aside every party distinction which can interfere with the present grand object, of arresting a danger so evident, so general, so imminent. It may be at first an awkward thing for Whig and Tory to draw kindly together; for any of the natural Scottish spirit which is left among us has been sadly expended in feeding a controversy in which we must always play a subordinate part, and these party distinctions have become far too much a matter of habit to us on both sides to be easily laid aside. Indeed, we poor Scotsmen are so conscious that our civil wars are but paltry and obscure episodes in the great political quarrel, that we have usually endeavoured to attract attention, and excite an idea of their importance, by the personal violence and noisy ferocity with which we wage them. We, the Whigs and Tories of Scotland, have played in our domestic quarrels the respectable part of two bull-dogs, who think it necessary to go by the ears under the table, because their blue-sleeved beef-eating masters have turned up for a set-to. The quadrupeds worry each other inveterately, while not a soul notices them till the strife of the bipeds is appeased or decided, and then the bleeding and foaming curs are kicked separate by their respective owners. We play among the great *dramatis personæ* the part of *Mob on both sides*, who enter and scuffle in the back scene, and shout so that their cries at least may be heard, since no one will attend to anything which they say in articulate language. You may have been a bottle-holder of this kind, Mr Journalist, to one or other of the great parties. I am sure I have, and I daresay may have sometimes made mischief, though I have oftener endeavoured to prevent it : for, like the good knight Jacques de Lalain, " *De feu bouter ne voulois-je etre consentant.* Still, however limited my share may have been in those jars, I have lived to see the day when I must regret bitterly my having had the slightest accession to them, could I conceive the opinions of so obscure an individual may have added gall to the bitterness which has estranged Scotsmen from each other. Let these follies be ended; and do not let us, like our ancestors at Falkirk, fall to jealousies among ourselves, when heart, and voice, and hand, should be united against the foreign *enemy*. I was about to eraze the last word; but let it remain, with this explanation—that the purpose of this invasion of our rights is acknowledged to be kind and friendly; but as the measure is unauthorized by justice, conducted without regard to the faith of treaties, and contrary to our national privileges, we cannot but term the enterprise a hostile one. When Henry VIII. dispatched a powerful invading army to compel the Scots to give the hand of their young Queen Mary to his son Edward, an old Scottish nobleman shrewdly observed, " He might like the match well enough, but could not brook the mode of wooing." We equally are sensible

of England's good will, we only do not relish
the mode in which it is at present exhibited.

The Scottish Members having thus adopted
a healing ordinance, reconciled their party quarrels, or laid them aside for the time, would by
that very act decide the fate of their country;
and when drinking to concord among Scotsmen
of all political opinions,

> In the cup an *Union* shall they throw
> Better than that which four successive kings
> In Britain's crown have worn.

Thus united, sir, their task will be a very easy
one. Let each, in his own style, and with the
degree of talent, from plain common sense up to
powerful eloquence, with which he chances to
be gifted, state to administration the sentiments
of his constituents, and those of his own breast;
let it be perfectly understood that the Representatives of Scotland speak in the name of their
country, and are determined, one and all, to see
the threatened and obnoxious measure departed
from, and till that time to enter into no public
business,—I cannot help thinking that such a
remonstrance, in a case of vital importance to
Scotland, and of such trifling consequence to

England, would be of itself perfectly sufficient.
But if not, our Representatives must stand firm.
I would advise that, to all such intimations as
are usually circulated, bearing, " That your presence is earnestly requested on such an evening
of the debate, as such or such a public measure
is coming on," the concise answer should be returned, " *We are five-and-forty;*" and that no
Scottish Members do on such occasions attend
—unless it be those who feel themselves conscientiously at liberty to vote against Government
on the division. Is this expecting too much
from our countrymen, on whom we have devolved so absolutely the charge of our rights, the
duty of stating our wrongs? We exclaim to them
in the language of the eloquent Lord Belhaven
—" Should not the memory of our noble predecessors' valour and constancy rouse up our droop-
ing spirits? Are our brave ancestors' souls got
so far into the English cabbage-stock and cau-
liflower, that we should show the least incli-
nation that way? Are our eyes so blinded—
Are our ears so deafened—Are our hearts so
hardened—Are our tongues so faltered—Are
our hands so fettered, that, in this our day—I

say, my countrymen, in this our day, we should not mind the things that concern the well-being, nay, the very being, of our ancient kingdom, before the day be hid from our eyes?" If there is, among that chosen band, a mean-spirited Scotsman, who prefers the orders of the Minister to the unanimous voice of his Country, imploring the protection of her children, let England keep him to herself. Such a man is deaf even to the voice of self-interest, as well as of patriotism. He cannot be a Scotch proprietor—he hazards his own rents ; he cannot be a Scotchman employed in commerce—he undermines his own trade ; he cannot be a professional person—he sacrifices the law of his country ; he cannot be a Scottish man in spirit—he betrays the honour of Scotland. Let him go out from among us—he is not of us. Let him, I say, remain in England, and we wish her joy of such a denizen. Let him have his title and his pension—for the cur deserves his collar and his bone. But do not let him come back to Scotland, where his presence will be as unwelcome to us, as our reception may be ungratifying to him.

It is needless to say, that what Scotland de-

mands from her representatives in the House of
Commons, she expects, with equal confidence and
ardour, from the small, but honourable portion
of the Upper House, who draw their honours
from her ancient domains. Their ancestors have
led her armies, concluded her treaties, managed
her government, served her with hand and heart,
sword and pen; and by such honourable merit
with their country, have obtained the titles and
distinctions which they have transmitted to the
present race, by whom, we are well assured, they
will be maintained with untarnished honour. A
Scottish Lord will dare all, save what is disho-
nourable; and whom among them could we suspect of deserting the Parent of his Honours, at
the very moment when she is calling upon him
for his filial aid? Sir, I pledge myself, ere I am
done, to give such a picture of the impending
distress of this country, that a Scotsman, and
especially a Scottish nobleman, would need to
take opium and mandragora, should he hope to
slumber, after having been accessary to bringing
it on. If the voice of the public in streets and
highways did not cry shame on his degeneracy,
even inanimate objects would find a voice of re-
probation. The stones of his ancient castle would

speak, and the portraits of his ancestors would
frown and look black upon him, as he wandered
in his empty halls, now deprived of the resort of
the rich, and the homage of the vassal. But I
have no fear of this. A little indolence—a little
indifference—may have spread itself among our
young men of rank ; it is the prevailing fashion
and fault of the day. But the trumpet of war
has always chased away such lethargic humours ;
and the cry of their common Country, that invo-
cation which Scotland now sends forth from one
end of the land to the other, is a summons yet
more imperious, and will be, I am confident, as
promptly obeyed.

It may be said, that the measures which I
venture to recommend to our Scottish representatives, of tacking, as it were, their Petition of
Rights, to every other measure, and making it,
so far as they can, a *sine quo non* to their accommodation with Government, may be the
means of interrupting the general business of
the empire.

To this objection I reply, *First*, that I only
recommend such a line of conduct as an *ultimum
remedium*, after every other and milder mode of
seeking redress shall have been resorted to, and

H

exhausted without effect. *Secondly,* In case of need it cannot be denied, that the plan proposed is a Parliamentary remedy, and corresponds with the conduct of patriots upon former occasions, when they conceived that the magnitude of the object in view warranted their making the most vigorous efforts to obtain it. *Thirdly,* It will not be difficult to demonstrate, that, whatever prejudice may be suffered from a temporary delay of other business, it will be incalculably less than the evil, which will infallibly ensue upon the obnoxious measure in question being adopted ; an evil, the effect of which cannot be confined to Scotland alone, (for no component part of the empire can have sufferings so local, that the consequences do not extend to the others,) but must reach England and Ireland also. When a limb of the human body is disjointed or broken, the whole frame must feel the effect of it.

But to return to the opinion of my cautious friends, who believed that the proportional numbers of the Scottish Members being so small, compared to those of England and Ireland, no good issue could be hoped from their exertions, however united, however zealous. I reply, that their country is entitled to expect

from them resistance in her behalf, not only
while a spark of hope remains, but when that
last spark is extinguished. There is no room for
compromise or surrender. Our statesmen of to-
day must be like our soldiers in ages past—

They must fight till their hand to the broadsword is glued,
They must fight against fortune with heart unsubdued.

If they do so, not only will they play the part
of true men and worthy patriots, but they will
procure that sort of weight with their constituents, which will enable them to be useful, and,
with the blessing of God, effectual mediators, in
what, I fear, is likely to prove a very distracted
time and country.

But besides this, I can tell my timorous
friends, as Hotspur does his cautious correspon-
dent,—" Out of this nettle Danger we pluck
the flower Safety." I do not think the Imperial
Parliament, consisting, as it now does, of depu-
ties from every kingdom of the Union, is so
likely to take a hasty and partial view of any
appeal from Scotland, as it might have been
when we had to plead our cause before the Parliament of Great Britain only. I trust we should
in no case have been treated unjustly or harshly,

and I will presently state my reasons for thinking that we should not ; but, arguing the question on the illiberal and almost calumnious idea,
that, if not confuted in argument, we were in
danger to be borne down by force of numbers, I
should derive hope, not fear, from the introduction of the third Kingdom into the discussion.

Betwixt Scotland and England, Mr Journalist, there have been, as you are aware, ancient
causes of quarrel, lulled to sleep during the last
fifty years, until of late, when a variety of small
aggressions, followed by the present seven-
leagued stride, show that perhaps they have not
been so fully forgotten by our neighbours, as we
thought in our simplicity, and that the English
Ministers may not be indisposed to take the opportunity of our torpidity to twitch out our fang-
teeth, however necessary for eating our victuals,
in case we should be inclined, at some unlucky
moment, to make a different use of them.   Or,
the line of conduct of which we complain, may
be compared to a well-known operation resorted
to for taming the ferocity of such male animals
as are intended for domestication, and to be employed in patient drudgery.   The animal becomes fat, patient, sleek, and in so far is bene-

fited by the operation; but had his previous consent been required, I wonder what the poor Scotch stot would have said?

Patrick, my warm-hearted and shrewd friend, how should you like this receipt for domestication, should it travel your way? You have your own griefs, and your own subjects of complaint,—are you willing to lose the power of expressing them with energy? You have only to join with the Ministry on this debate—you have only to show in what light reverence you are willing to hold the articles of an Union not much above a century old, and then you will have time to reflect at leisure upon the consequences of such an example. In such a case, when your turn comes, (and come be sure it will,) you will have signed your own sentence. You will have given the fatal precedent to England of the annihilation of a solemn treaty of incorporating Union, and afforded the representatives of Scotland vindictive reasons for retaliating upon you the injury which you aided England in inflicting upon us. Whereas—step this way, Pat—and see there is nobody listening—why should not you and we have a friendly understanding, and assist each other, as the weaker

parties, against any aggressions, which may be
made upon either of us, "for uniformity's sake?"
—Your fathers are called by our Scottish Kings,
" Their ancient friends of the Erischerie of Eir-
land," and for my part I have little doubt that
Malachi, who wore the collar of gold, must have
been an ancestor of my own.   Now, what say
you to a league offensive and defensive, against
all such measures as tend to the suppression of
any just right belonging to either country, in
virtue of the Articles of Union respectively?—
You are a scholar, Pat—

" *Tua res agitur, proxima cum paries ardet.*"

Between ourselves, Patrick, John Bull is, not
unnaturally, desirous of having rather more than
his own share in managing the great national
coach-and-six. He will drive four-in-hand; and
though he has hitherto allowed you a postilion
of your own, yet in some scheme of economy he
may dismiss him if you do not look sharp, and
drive the whole set of six horses himself. It is
different portions of their ancient independence
which are reserved to Scotland and Ireland by
their respective treaties of Union. Scotland retained her ancient laws, and Ireland a typical

representation of her national sovereignty. But
both rights are held by the same tenure, and
if Ireland set an example, by aiding a gross in-
fringement of the Scottish Union—if she aid
England, in destroying for mere humour—I
beg pardon, for mere " uniformity's sake,"—
every little mark of independence which is left
us—if she countenance the obvious desire which
exhibits itself to break down all peculiar privileges due to the separate nations of the Union,
to engross the whole management in Boards,
which, sitting in London, and begirt by Englishmen, are to dispense the patronage, and
direct the improvements, of another nation
of the Union, Ireland will accelerate her own
then unpitied degradation. What is our case
to-day, brothers of Erin, will be yours the instant you have got a little tranquillity—are
caught napping—and are in condition to have
the aforesaid ceremony practised upon you without danger—I mean danger to the operator, for
peril to the creature itself is of no consequence.
I see you grasp your shilela at the very thought !
Enough ; we understand each other : Let us be
friends. Patrick aids Saunders to-day ; Saunders pays back Patrick to-morrow, or I will

throw away my thistle, burn my St Andrew's cross, and disclaim my Country!

But what do I talk of to-day or to-morrow? The cause of Ireland is tried ALONG WITH that of Scotland. She stands, at this very moment, at the bar beside her Sister, and the prohibitory decree passed against the system of currency, which has spread universal fertility through Scotland, is extended to Ireland at the very moment when she proposed to have recourse to it, as well suited to the improvement of her rich soil, and promising the extension of means of cultivation, where cultivation is so greatly wanted, and would be so productive in the return. I am certain that I am correct in saying, that, in the course of last summer, there were several Banking Companies on the Scottish plan on the point of being established in different parts of Ireland, and Scotsmen of experience, capable of understanding and directing such establishments, were eagerly sought for, and invited over to act as superintendants. Whether the system which had been so eminently successful in Scotland might be found quite as well qualified for the meridian of Ireland, it would be great presumption in me to decide. But it is very likely that success

would ensue, provided too much were not expected at once, and that the requisite discretion
were used in bounding the issue of notes, and
the grants of credit. More or less probable, it
was at least an experiment which Ireland had
apparently a perfect right to make, an experiment by which she might reasonably hope to
profit ; and if she was willing to undertake it at
her own risk, I can conceive nothing more unjust
than preventing her from doing so—excepting
always the still greater iniquity of interdicting
in Scotland a system, the benefit of which has
been proved by a century's experience, during
all which period it has been attended with advantage, but in the last fifty years with the most
brilliant success.

Ireland is therefore called upon to interfere
on this occasion, not merely by the chance of
standing, at some no very distant period, in the
very predicament in which Scotland is now
placed, but from the stake which she herself has
in the question at issue. She cannot but remember that Rome subjected the free states
around her much less by the force which was
actually her own, than by the use which she
made of those whom she had rendered her tools

under the name of auxiliaries. The Batavians were employed in the conquest of Britain, the flower of the Britons were carried off from their native country, that they might help to subjugate the Germans. But such a policy, were it entertained, is not likely to deceive nations in the present age, when statesmen are judged of not more by the measure which they mete to countries less capable of resistance, than by that which they use in dealing towards one upon whom it may not be immediately convenient to inflict the same unjust terms.

Ireland may read her future fate in that of Scotland, as in a mirror. Does she still continue to entertain any wish of imitating the Scottish system? the measure of interdiction about to be passed against her renders it impossible.—Does she still expect to be occasionally consulted in the management of her own affairs? She may lay aside for ever that flattering hope, unless she makes common cause with her sister of Scotland, where every human being in the nation is entreating and imploring that dearest privilege of a free country.—Finally, let us have a word of explanation with England herself.

And first let me say, that although the urgent

necessity of the case requires that it should be pleaded in every possible form which its advocates can devise—although I press upon Scotland the necessity of being importunate, steady, and unanimous—although I show to Ireland the deep interest which she also must feel in the question at issue, yet it is to England herself, and to her representatives in Parliament, that, taking upon me, however unworthy, to speak for my Country, when the task is perhaps an obnoxious one, I make my most immediate, and I trust not an ineffectual appeal.

The motto of my epistle may sound a little warlike ; but, in using it,* I have only employed the summons which my countrymen have been best accustomed to obey. Saunders, if it please your honours, has been so long unused to stand erect in your honours' presence, that, if I would have him behave like a man, I must (like Sir Lucius O'Trigger backing Bob Acres) slap him on the shoulder, and throw a word in every now

---

* It was the following verse of an old song :—

> When the pipes begin to play
> *Tutti taittic* to the drum,
> Out claymore, and down wi' gun,
> And to the rogues again !

I have laid it aside in this edition, some cautious friends thinking it liable to misinterpretation.

and then about his *honour*. But it is not a hostile signal towards you. The drums beat *to arms* and the trumpets sound *Heraus,* as well when the soldiers are called out for a peaceful as for a military object. And, which is more to the purpose, the last time the celebrated Fiery Cross was circulated in the Highlands, (it was in the country of the Grants,) the clansmen were called forth not to fight an enemy, but to stop the progress of a dreadful conflagration which had been kindled in the woods. To my countrymen I speak in the language of many recollections, certain they are not likely to be excited beyond the bounds of temperate and constitutional remonstrance, but desirous, by every effort in my power, to awaken them to a sense of their national danger.

England—were it mine to prescribe the forms, my native country ought to address nearly in the words of her own Mason, mangled, I fear, in my recollection—

> " Sister, to thee no ruder spell
> Will Scotland use, than those that dwell
> In soft Persuasion's notes, and lie
> Twined with the links of *Harmony*."

Let us, therefore, my countrymen, make a pro-

per and liberal allowance for the motives of the
Ministers and their friends on this occasion. We
ought not to be surprised that English statesmen, and Englishmen in general, are not altogether aware of the extent of the Scottish privileges, or that they do not remember, with the
same accuracy as ourselves, that we have a system of laws peculiar to us, secured by treaties.
These peculiarities have not, by any question
lately agitated, been placed under their view
and recollection. As one race grows up, and
another dies away, remembrances which are che-
rished by the weaker party in a national treaty,
are naturally forgotten by the stronger, and
viewed, perhaps, as men look upon an old bound-
ary stone, half-sunk in earth, half-overgrown
with moss, and attracting no necessary attention,
until it is appealed to as a proof of property.
Such antiquated barriers are not calculated immediately to arrest the progress of statesmen in-
tent upon some favourite object, any more than,
when existing on the desolate mountain in their
physical shape, such a bound-mark as I have described, always checks the eagerness of a stranger
upon the moors, in keen and close pursuit of his
game. But explain to the ardent young Southern sportsman that he trespasses upon the manor

of another—convince the English statesman that
he cannot advance his favourite object without
infringing upon national right,—and, according
to my ideas of English honour and good faith,
the one will withdraw his foot within the bound-
ary of private property, with as much haste as if
he trod on burning marle ; the other will curb
his views of public good, and restrain even those
within the limits which are prescribed by public
faith.   They will not, in either case, forget the
precepts so often reiterated in Scripture, fenced
there with a solemn anathema, and received as
matter of public jurisprudence by the law of
every civilized country—" Remove not the old
land-mark, and enter not into the fields of the
fatherless."   The high and manly sense of justice by which the English nation has been honourably distinguished through the world, will
not, I am certain, debase itself by aggression towards a people, which is not indeed incapable of
defending itself, but which, though fearless of
inequality, and regardless of threats, is yet willing to submit even to wrong, rather than hazard the fatal consequences to be incurred by
obstinate defence, *via facti*, of its just rights.
We make the sense of English justice and
honour our judge ; and surely it would be hard

to place us in a situation where our own sense of general mischief likely to ensue to the empire, may be the only check upon the sentiments which brave men feel, when called on to defend their national honour. There would be as little gallantry in such an aggression, as in striking a prisoner on parole.

It is to explain more particularly to the English nation, the real and deep reason which Scotland has to combat the present purpose of Ministers, that I have chiefly undertaken this Second Epistle.

I have stated in my former Letter, that the system respecting the currency, which is now about to be abrogated, has been practised in Scotland for about one hundred and thirty years, with the greatest advantage to the country and inhabitants. I have also shown from the Treaty of Union, that it cannot be altered, unless the preliminary is established to the conviction of Parliament, that the alteration is for the EVIDENT ADVANTAGE *of the subjects in Scotland.* No advantage, evident or remote, has ever been hinted at, so far as Scotland is concerned : it has only been said, that it will be advantageous to England, to whose measures Scotland must be

conformable, as a matter of course, though in
the teeth of the article stipulated by our Commissioners, and acceded to by those of England,
at the time of the Union. I have therefore
gained my cause in any fair Court.

But protesting that I have done enough to
entitle me to a judgment, I have no objection to
go a step farther; and, taking on myself a burthen
of proof, which could not be justly imposed on
me, I am willing to explain in a general and
popular manner the peculiar nature of the paper
currency in Scotland, and especially the guards
and protections by which it is secured against
such evil consequences as have resulted in England from a system the same in name, but operating very differently in practice.

The people of Scotland are by no means, as
a hasty view of their system of currency might
infer, liable to be imposed upon, or to suffer loss,
through the rash and crude speculations of any
man, or association of men, who, without adequate capital and experience, might choose to
enter into a Banking concern, and issue their
own notes.

The Banking Companies of Scotland, who
take on themselves the issuing of notes, are, no

doubt, independent of each other so far as they severally contract with the public; but a certain course of correspondence and mutual understanding is indispensable among themselves, and, in that respect, the whole Banks and Banking Companies in Scotland may be said to form a republic, the watchful superintendence of the whole profession being extended to the strength or weakness of the general system at each particular point ; or, in other words, to the management of each individual Company.

No new Banking institution can venture to issue notes to the public, till they have established a full understanding that these notes will be received as cash by the other Banks. Without this facility, an issue of notes would never take place, since, if issued, they could have no free or general currency. It is not the interest of the established Banks to raise rivals in their own profession, and it is directly contrary to that interest to accept of payment in the notes of a new Company, to whose responsibility there occurs any shadow of doubt. They, therefore, only agree to give currency to such new issues, where satisfactory information has been obtained of the safety of affording it. The public have, in this

I

manner, the best possible guarantee against rash
and ill-concocted speculations, from those who
are not only best informed on the subject, but,
being most interested in examining each new
project of the kind, are least likely to be betray-
ed into a rash confidence, and have the power of
preventing a doubtful undertaking at the very
outset.

The circulation of a Scottish Banking Company, when once established, cannot maintain
itself a week without redeeming its pledge to
the Banks which receive its notes, by taking
them up, and replacing the value either in the
notes of such Banks reciprocally, or in specie.
A check is thus imposed, which is continually
in operation, and every Bank throughout Scotland is obliged to submit its circulation, twice
a-week, in Edinburgh, to the inspection of this
Argus-eyed tribunal.   Satisfactory information
that any distant Banking Companies were leaving
the safe and moderate walk of commerce, and
embarking their capital in precarious speculations, would very soon draw upon them the suspicion of the moneyed interest at large, and certainly put a period to their existence before it
could injure the public.

This important species of check is unknown

to the practice of England ; nay, it is probably impossible to establish it there, since the metropolis, which is naturally the common point of union, is nearly inaccessible to the notes of private Banking Companies. In stating a circumstance, not perhaps generally known, I may perhaps remove some of the prejudice which has extended towards the Scottish system, as if exposed to the same inconveniencies with that of the sister kingdom.

The Cash-Credits, as they are called, are a most important feature in our Banking system, and, as I believe, entirely peculiar to it.

The nature of the transaction is the simplest possible. A person, either professional, engaged in commerce or manufactures, or otherwise so situated as to render an occasional command of money convenient, obtains a Cash Account to an extent proportioned to his funds, either by pledging his house, shop, or other real property, or by giving the Bank two sufficient sureties to be answerable for the balance, if any, which shall be due to the Company when the Account is closed. The holder of the Cash-Credit is then entitled to draw on the Banker for such sums as he may occasionally need, within its limits. He lodges, on the other hand, with the Bank, such cash as he may from time to time receive from the returns of his business, or otherwise. Interest is calculated on the advances drawn from the Bank at five per cent, on the customer's deposits at three per cent only, and the account is finally balanced twice a-year. The interest varies according to the general rate of the money-market. I have stated it upon the general and legal rate, which it never does or can exceed.

This very simple accommodation is so general through Scotland, that no undertaking of the slightest magnitude is entered into without sufficient funds being provided in this manner, in order that the expense may be maintained without inconvenience until the profits come round. By means of such credits, the merchant carries on his trade, the agriculturist manages his farm, the professional man discharges the advances necessary in his business, and the landed gentleman maintains his credit, and pays his way, while waiting for the tardy return of his rents. The trustees who conduct public works have recourse to the same accommodation. Scarce any one who is not too rich to need an occasional advance, (a case very rare in Scotland,) or too poor to obtain credit, but is provided and acts upon some Cash Account of this kind, being a sort of fluctuating system of borrowing and lending. In the former case, the customer borrows of the Bank the advances which he needs, in such sums and at such times as they are necessary ; whereas, without such mutual accommodation, the loan must have been borrowed in an entire sum, and paid up at once, though in the former case it included more money than was immediately wanted ; and, in the latter, the settlement of the whole demand at once might be untimely and inconvenient.

Supposing the money lodged to exceed the amount of the credit, the customer becomes a creditor to the Banker for the balance due to him, and receives a stated interest for it ; while, at the same time, it lies, as in an ordinary deposit account, at his immediate command. This system is, no doubt, liable, like everything earthly, to abuse. But the general prosperity of the country, managed almost entirely on such an arrangement betwixt those who deal in capital, and those who need the use of it, has shown that the partial abuse bears no proportion to the universal advantage. The system has, in its exercise, been, as Shakspeare says of Mercy, " *twice blessed.*" It has prospered both with the giver and the taker ; and while the holder of the Account has been enabled to derive wealth from schemes which he could not otherwise have executed, the increasing funds of the Banker, and his additional power of serving the country, and aiding, in similar instances, the progress of general improvement, add to the sum of national riches.

It is also to be observed, that the intimate connexion between the Bankers who grant, and the respectable individuals who hold cash-credits, from L.100 to L.1000 and upwards, tends greatly to the security of the former. These customers, of whom each thriving Bank possesses many, are the chief holders and disposers of notes ; and, linked as they are with the Banks who grant the accommodation, by mutual advantage, they have both the interest and credit necessary to quash any unreasonable alarm, and secure the Company against what is called a Run, a circumstance to which Scottish Banks have never been materially exposed, and which is not very consistent with the character of the people.

These undeniable facts afford, so far as Scotland is concerned, a decisive confutation to an argument which has been advanced, for abroga-

ting the issue of small notes. It has been alleged, that such issues being chiefly in the hands
of the lower classes, these were agitated easily
by rumours, and they became the occasion of the
Runs above-mentioned, by which the Banking
Companies are ruined ; as men are crushed to
death in a crowd, when those around them are
agitated by some cause, very likely a vain one,
of panic terror. In itself, it seems, that depriving men of a lucrative branch of their profession, merely because, under certain circumstances, it may become dangerous to their stability, is very like the receipt of Sheepface in the
farce, who kills his master's sheep to prevent their
dying. But, in Scotland, there exists not the
least approach to the disease, which it seems
necessary to anticipate in so desperate a manner ;
for the apprehended *Runs* on Scotch Banks, by
the holders of small notes, have never taken
place, and, from the assigned reasons, are never
likely to do so. But should such an event occur,
the interference of the Banks' customers, parties
so much interested, would stop such a headlong
movement, as a strong and well-ordered police
would prevent the fatal agitations of a mob, ere
they trod each other to death.

The general principle of the Credits thus

granted, is one which, in a poor country at least, or among poor traders, is highly desirable. It affords the farmer, trader, or country gentleman, a convenient and equitable means of pledging their property for a fund of credit to conduct their undertakings. It resembles in principle, though on a much more equitable and liberal footing, the impignoration of moveables, which affords facilities, without which the small, yet indispensable branches of traffic, could not be carried on. Let us, in due humility, follow out a comparison at which our pride might be justly revolted. In London, and other great cities, the market-women, and persons of that description, are constantly in the practice of raising a small credit, by pledging their little articles of value, whether ornaments or wearing apparel, or the like, on which they maintain their trade till Saturday brings the weekly returns, when the ornaments are redeemed from the pawnbrokers, worn perhaps on the Sunday, and returned to *lavender* (as the phrase goes) on the next Monday. It is now many years since some well-disposed and benevolent persons, becoming aware of this practice, were shocked and scandalized at the extent of the interest exacted from these poor people, and made or proposed a law for rendering this course of pawnbroking illegal. Sir, the general mass of misery which was about to attend on the well-meant interference of the legislature, was so evident and so alarming, that the measure was either departed from ere it was completed, or repealed immediately, I forget which.

Paullo majora—The principle is in effect the very same on which, to restore public credit, the Bank of England itself is about to advance three millions of money on the security of mercantile commodities.

In the same way, we have in Scotland got into the regular habit of pledging our credit in the manner above described, for the purpose of raising a disposable capital. The advantage obtained by both parties is very equitably balanced; but, were it as iniquitous as that of the most grinding pawnbroker, still habit and manners have rendered it absolutely indispensable to us; and, when a general source of credit is forcibly snatched from a country which has relied on it so long, you literally wrest the crutch from the infirm, because, in your mind, it is not of a handsome fashion.

After all, is it not just that we, the party concerned, should be admitted to have a preponderating vote in this matter? If we are eventually losing by adhering to an old and tried system, we can blame no one, but must suffer for our own obstinacy; but if Scotland is to be reduced to distress by having a system forced upon her which she is unable to maintain or carry on, who is to answer for the evils it may bring upon us?

It is by the profit arising upon issuing their small notes, that the Bankers are enabled to make the beneficial advances which custom has now rendered nearly indispensable to the carrying on business of almost any kind in Scotland. Above all, without that profit, the Bankers could not, as hitherto, continue to allow a rateable interest on money deposited in their hands. Let us take a hasty view of some of the advantages attached to this peculiarity of the system.

The general convenience of the Banker affording interest upon deposits is obvious. It is much more convenient to the individual to receive some interest for his ready cash, than that it should lie idle in his desk; and its being thus put into a productive state, instead of remaining an unproductive capital must be much more useful to the country. This needs no commentary.

It has, besides, tended much to the diminution of crime in Scotland. We have forgot the period preceding the Banking system, but it is easily recalled. Look at the old magazines or newspapers, during the time when the currency was chiefly maintained by specie, a ready temptation to the ruffian—the murder of graziers and dealers returning from fairs where they had sold their cattle, was a not infrequent occurrence. Farm-houses of the better class, as well as gentlemen's baronial residences, were defended by bars on the windows, upper and under, like those of a prison ; yet these houses were often broken open by daring gangs, to possess themselves of the hoards which the tenant must have then kept beside him against rent-day, and his landlord, for the current expense of his household. At present—*Cantabit vacuus*—the drover or grazier has a Banker's receipt for the price of his cattle, in the old almanack which serves him for a pocket-book, and fears no robbery—while the farm-house, or manor, is secure from the attack of ruffians, who are like to find no metal there more precious than the tongs and poker.

Passing over the tendency of the present sys-

tem to prevent crime, I come to its influence in
recommending industry and virtue ; and I am
confident in stating, that the degree of morali-
ty, sobriety, and frugality, which is admitted
to exist in Scotland, has been much fostered,
though certainly not entirely produced, by the
Banks' allowing interest on small sums, which,
if the present prohibitory measure passes, they
will be no longer in a capacity to afford. Let
the effect of such a violent change be considered
merely in respect to the lowest order of deposi-
tors, who lodge in the Bank from the sum of
ten pounds to fifty. The first motive to save,
among petty tradesmen, mechanics, farm-ser-
vants, domestics, and the like, is the delight of
forming a productive capital ; and in that class,
the habit of saving and of frugality is the foundation of a sober, well-regulated, and useful society. Every judicious farmer scruples to repose
perfect reliance in a farm-servant or a labourer,
till he knows that he is possessed of a capital of
a few pounds in some neighbouring Bank ; and
when that is once attained, the man becomes
tenfold steady and trustworthy. Instances have
occurred, to my certain knowledge, before the
time of the Saving-Banks, where the master,

to hasten this advantageous step in his dependent's life, would advance a servant of character
a little money to complete a deposit, when the
man's savings did not amount to ten pounds,
which is the least sum received by the Banks.
And, by the way, it is not easy to see how these
excellent institutions, the Saving-Banks themselves, can be continued in Scotland, if interest
is no longer allowed by the general Bank ; for
we are at too great a distance to avail ourselves
of the Public Funds for that purpose.

At any rate, the cessation of payment of interest by the Banks, attendant on the abolish-
ing the issue of small notes, would greatly injure, if not effectually destroy, the formation of
those virtuous and frugal habits, which are as
essential to the class of society a little richer
than that to which the Saving-Banks apply, as
to the inferior description to whom these invaluable institutions afford encouragement and
protection.

What is a poor hind or shepherd to do with his
L.20 or L.30, the laborious earnings of his life,
and which he looks to, under God, for keeping
his widow and family from the parish, if Bankers
can no longer afford him some interest for the

use of it ? Where is he to get decent security
for his petty capital ? He will either be swin-
dled out of it by some rascally attorney, or coax-
ed to part with it to some needy relation—in
either case, never to see it more. It is difficult
enough, even at present, for masters, who take
an interest in their servants' welfare, to get them
to place their money safe in the Bank ; if this
resource is taken away, where is it to be lodged,
with any chance of security ? But I think I can
guess its fate, friend Journalist. The Banks will
be forcing back on the hands of the shepherd
or farm-servant his deposit, just at the time when
they are unwillingly distressing his master for the
balance on his Cash Account, called up before his
well-judged, but half-executed improvements,
undertaken on the faith of the continued credit,
have become productive. The farmer will, in
the hour of need and pressure, borrow the petty
capital of his servant ; he will be unable to repay it ; and then, when the distress becomes
chin-deep, they may turn beggars together—for
uniformity's sake.

If that settling day should ever come, Mr
Journalist, when the Bankers, dunned for deposits in their hands, are compelled to be as

rigorous with those who have received advances from them—that awful day, when the hundreds of thousands, nay millions, hitherto divided between the Banks and the Public, must be all called up at once, and accounts between them closed—that settling day will be remembered as long in Scotland as ever was the Mirk Monday!

But what can the Bankers do? Their whole profession must undergo a universal change, that discounts and every species of accommodation may be brought within the narrowest possible limits. At present, the profits divided among the profession, upon perhaps a Million and a Half of small notes, enable them to advance liberally to individuals upon any reasonable security. But if the Banker's occupation is henceforth to consist in stocking himself with a great abundance of gold, and for that purpose engaging in an eternal struggle, not to *preserve* (for that is impossible), but to *restore* an eternally vacillating proportion betwixt the metallic circulation and the wants of the country, such expensive labour ALONE will be likely to prove quite enough for his talents and funds.

The injury done to the Bankers, by depriving

them of such a principal and profitable branch of their profession, is not to be passed over in silence. The English are wont, in other cases, to pay particular heed ere they alter any peculiar state of things, upon the faith of which property has been vested in a fixed and permanent line of employment. But this proposed enactment will go as far as the in-calling of One Million and a Half of notes can do, to destroy the emoluments of the profession. You deprive them of those very notes which travel farthest from home, and which return most slowly; nay, which, from various causes, are subject not to return at all. It is therefore in vain to say that thus the profession is left uninjured, when it is limited to the issue of notes of five pounds and upwards. It might be as reasonably stated in a case of mutilation, that a man was left in the entire and uninjured possession of his hand, the prisoner having only cut off his five fingers.

If, therefore, the proposed measure shall take place, the Bankers' profession must suffer greatly, nay, in its present form, must cease to exist. We cannot, as a nation, afford to be deprived of such an honourable and profitable means of settling our sons in the world. We cannot afford to lose a resource, which has proved to so many respectable and honourable families a means *ad reædificandum antiquam domum,* and which has held out to others a successful mode of elevating themselves, by liberal and useful industry, to the possession of wealth, at once to their own advantage and to that of Scotland. Thus it must needs be, if the proposed measure should pass ; and when we come to count the gains we shall then have made, by change from a paper circulation to one in specie, I doubt it will form a notable example of the truth of the proverb, " *That gold may be bought too dear.*"

The Branches established by Banks in remote parts of Scotland must be given up. The parent Banks would vainly exhaust themselves in endeavouring to draw specie from London, and to force it, at whatever expense, into more fertile districts of Scotland, which, of course, would receive it in small quantity, and pay for it at a heavy charge. But as to the remote and sterile regions, it must be with the Highlands and Isles of Scotland, as it is now in some remote districts of Ireland, where scarce any specie exists for the purpose of ordinary currency, and where, for want of that representative for value

K

or paper money in its stead, men are driven back
to the primitive mode of bartering for everything
—the peasant pays his rent in labour, and the
fisher gets his wages in furnishings. Misery is
universal—credit is banished—and with all the
bounties of nature around them, ready to reward
industry—the sinews of that industry are hewn
asunder, and man starves where Nature has
given abundance!

Great Britain would be then somewhat like
the image in Belteshazzar's dream. London, its
head, might be of fine gold—the fertile provinces
of England, like its breast and arms, might be of
silver—the southern half of Scotland might ac-
quire some brass or copper—but the northern
provinces would be without worth or value, like
the legs, which were formed of iron and clay.
What force is to compel gold to circulate to
these barren extremities of the island, I cannot
understand ; and, when once forced there, I fear
its natural tendency to return to the source from
which it is issued will render all efforts to detain
it as difficult as the task of the men of Gotham,
when they tried to hedge in the cuckoo. Our
Bankers, or such as may continue in the profession under the same name, but with very differ-

ent occupation and prospects, will be condemned to the labour of Sisyphus,—eternally employed in rolling a cask of gold up a Highland hill, at the risk of being crushed by it as the influence of gravity prevails, and it comes rolling down upon their heads.

Mrs Primrose, wife to the excellent Vicar of Wakefield, carried on a system of specie, with respect to her family, at a much cheaper rate than that at which Scotland will be able, I fear, to accomplish the same object. " I gave each of them a shilling," says the good man, speaking of his daughters, " though for the honour of the family it must be observed, that they never went without money themselves ; as my wife always generously let them have a guinea each to keep their pockets, but with strict injunctions *never to change it.*" Our state is not so favourable, Mr Journalist. We shall be obliged to lay out our guinea every morning of our lives, and to buy back another every evening, at an increasing per céntage, to pay the expense of the next day. Moreover, Mrs Primrose was more reasonable (begging pardon for the expression) than our English friends ; for, although she enforced the specie system in her own family, we do not hear

that she was ever desirous to intrude it into that
of Neighbour Flamborough.

I do not mean to enter into the general question of the difference betwixt the circulation of
specie and of paper money. I speak of them re-
latively, as applicable to the wants and wishes
of Scotland only. Yet, I must say, it seems
strange, that, under a liberal system, of which
freedom of trade is the very soul, we should be
loaded with severe restrictions upon our own national choice, instead of being left at liberty to
adopt that representative of value, whether in
gold or paper, that best suits our own convenience !

To return to the remote Highlands and Is-
lands, Mr Journalist, I need not tell you that
they are inhabited by a race of men, to use Dr
Currie's phrase, " patient of labour and prodigal
of life," for succouring whose individual wants
the tenth part of an English coal-heaver's wages
would be more than enough, but yet who are
human creatures, and cannot live absolutely
without food—who are men, and entitled to
human compassion—Christians, and entitled to
Christian sympathy. But their claims as men
and Christians are not all they have to proffer

to administration and to England. The distress
to which they are about to be exposed will return
upon the state at large in a way very little con-
templated.

Those sterile and remote regions have been
endowed by Providence with treasures of their
own, gained from the stormy deep by their hardy
inhabitants. The fisheries in the distant Highlands and Isles, under the management of an
enlightened Board, have at length accomplished
what was long the warmest wish of British patriots, and have driven the Dutch out of all ri-
valry in this great branch of national industry.
The northern fisheries furnish exports to our colonies and to the Continent, exceeding half a
million of money annually, and give employment to a very great number of hardy seamen.
The value of such a plentiful source of prosperity, whether considered as supplying our navy
or affecting our manufactures, is sufficiently obvious. Now observe, Mr Journalist, how these
fisheries are at present conducted.

The branches of those obnoxious establishments, the Scottish Banks, maintained at convenient and centrical points in the north of
Scotland, furnish all the remote and numerous

stations where the fisheries are carried on, with small notes and silver for payment of the actual fishers' labour, and in return accept the bills of the fish-curers upon the consignees. This they do at a moderate profit ; on which principle alone private industry, and enterprise, and capital, can be made conducive to the public good. The small notes thus circulated in the most distant parts of Scotland, return, indeed, in process of time, to the Banks which issued them ; but the course of their return is so slow and circuitous, that the interest accruing on them during their absence amply reimburses the capitalist for the trouble and risk which attend the supply. But let any man who knows the country, or will otherwise endeavour to conceive its poverty and sterility, imagine if he can, the difficulties, expense, and hazard, at which gold must be carried to points where it would never have voluntarily circulated, and from whence, unless detained in some miser's hoard, (a practice which the currency in specie, and disuse of interest on deposits, is likely to revive,) it will return to London with the celerity of a carrier-pigeon.

The manufacture of Kelp, which is carried

on to an immense extent through all the shores
and Isles of the Highlands, supporting thousands
of men with their families, who must otherwise
emigrate or starve, and forming the principal
revenue of many Highland proprietors, is nearly, if not exactly, on the same footing with the
fisheries ; is carried on chiefly by the same medium of circulation ; and, like them, supplied by
the Bankers with small notes for that purpose, at a reasonable profit to themselves, and
with the utmost advantage to the country and
its productive resources.

Referring once more to the state of misery
in the distant districts of Ireland, I must once
more ask, if these things be done in the green
tree, what shall be done in the dry tree? If the
want of circulation creates poverty and misery
in the comparatively fertile country of Ireland,
what is to become of those barren deserts, where
even at present the hardest labour which the human frame can endure is necessary to procure
the most moderate pittance on which human life
can be supported ? The inhabitants are now heal-
thy, enterprising, laborious ; and their industry,
producing means of existence to themselves, is
of immense profit to their country. If their

means of obtaining the payment of their labour is destroyed, nay even interrupted, the state must either feed idle paupers, who once flourished a hardy and independent race of labourers, or it must be at the expense of transporting the inhabitants to Canada and New South Wales, and leaving totally waste a country, which few but those bound to it by the *Amor patriæ* will desire to reside in, even if the means of procuring subsistence were left unimpaired.

Can anything short of the UTMOST NECESSITY justify an experiment, which threatens to depopulate a part of the empire, and destroy the happiness of thousands ? and how can such a necessity exist, without the least symptom of its having been felt or suspected during the last hundred and thirty years, when the present system has been in exercise ?

Destroy the existing conduit, and let me again inquire, what forcing-pump, what new-invented patent pressure, were it devised by Bramah himself, is to compel specie into those inaccessible regions ? The difficulty of conveying the supplies is augmented by the risk of carrying wealth unguarded through the regions of poverty. I know my countrymen are indifferent

honest, as Hamlet says ; yet I would not advise the Genius of the specie system to travel
through Scotland, moral as the country is, after
the fashion of the fair pilgrim, " rich and rare,"
in Moore's beautiful melody, just by way of trying the integrity of the inhabitants. Take my
word for it, the absence of temptation is no valueless guardian of virtue. If convoys of gold must
be sent through lonely mountains, I venture to
say, that smugglers will be converted into robbers, and that our romance-writers need not
turn back to ancient times for characters like
John Gunn, or Rob Roy Macgregor.

This I am sure of, that if the mere authority
of a legislative enactment can force a sufficient
quantity of gold into those parts, to carry on the
fishery and kelp manufactures, it can do a great
deal more in favour of the poor but hardy inhabitants. Why should our statesmen be so stint-
ed in their bounty, if it depends merely on legislative enactment ? Why not enact, that whereas the dress now worn by his Majesty's loving
inhabitants of the Lewis, Uist, Harries, Eddera-
chyles, Cape-Wrath, and Loch Horrible, is scan-
ty, thin, and indecorous, each inhabitant of those
districts should in future wear a full-trimmed
suit of black silk, or velvet ; and, as his only

representative of wealth has been hitherto a crumpled dog's-ear'd piece of Scotch paper, that, in future, he never presume to stir out of his cabin without having, and bearing about his person, the sum of at least five golden sovereigns? The working the stuffs may be a means of relieving the starving weavers of Spitalfields, and the clothes could be conveniently enough forwarded by the escorts who are to protect the chests of specie.

It is not amiss to observe that this violent experiment on our circulation—demanded by no party in Scotland—nay, forced upon us against the consent of all who can render a reason, fraught with such deep ruin if it miscarry, and holding forth no prospect whatever of good even should it prove successful,—can only be carried on at a very considerable expense to England. She must coin for the service of Scotland at least a million and a half of specie—sustain the loss of tear and wear—the chance of accident and plunder—of disappearance by pilfering and hoarding—and be at the expense of supplying this immense quantity of precious metals, not for the benefit, but for the probable ruin, of our devoted country. It is fairly forcing gold down our throats, as little to our advantage, as when the precious metal was sent in a molten state down the gullet of Cyrus, or Crassus,—I forget which.

No argument has been alleged by the English statesmen for pressing this measure, but that of " uniformity ;" by virtue of which principle, a little more extended, they may introduce the Irish Insurrection Law into England to-morrow, and alter the whole national law of Scotland the day after. This argument, I therefore think, proves a little too much, and is, in consequence, no argument at all. In absence of avowed motives, and great darkness as to any imaginable cause, men's minds have entertained very strange and wild fancies, to account for the zeal with which this obnoxious measure is driven forward. Some, who would be thought to see farther into a mill-stone than others, pretend the real reason is to soothe the jealousy of the Bank of England, by preventing the possibility of Scots notes passing in England. It is easy to see how people must be puzzled to discover the semblance of a possible motive, when they have recourse to such figments as this. Can it be conceived that our dearest interests are to be tampered with for such an object ?— It is very true, that in the adjacent counties of

England, innkeepers for courtesy, and drovers and others dealing at Scots fairs, on account of convenience, readily accept of Scots notes in payment; but that notes, which nobody is obliged to accept, and which the English Banks refuse to change, can circulate to such an extent as to alarm the Bank of England!—why, sir, I will as soon believe, that, during the old wars, the city of London beat to arms, called out their Trained-bands, and manned their walls, because the Teviotdale Borderers had snapped up a herd of cattle in Northumberland. What becomes of the comparative excellence of the specie circulation to be established in England, if apprehensions are entertained that it cannot stand its ground against the reprobated paper system of Scotland? In God's name, are they afraid people will prefer paper to gold—leaving, like Hamlet's misjudging mother, the literally golden meads of England, to batten on a Scottish moor? It is like the ridiculous story told, that there is a bye-law, or at least a private understanding, that no Scotsman shall be chosen a Director of the Bank of England, lest our countrymen engross the whole management in the course of a few years.—Why, sir, these opinions remind one of the importance attached to the fated Stone in Westminster Abbey, of which it is said, that the Scots shall reign wheresoever it is carried. But, sir, we must not swallow such flattering compliments. The Bank of England jealous of the partial circulation of a few Scottish notes in the north of England ! ! ! Sir, it would be supposing the blessed sun himself jealous of a gas-light manufactory.

A few general observations on England's late conduct to us, and I will release you.

A very considerable difference may be remarked, within these twenty-five years, in the conduct of the English towards such of the Scotch individuals, as either visit the metropolis as mere birds of passage, or settle there as residents. Times are much changed since the days of Wilkes and Liberty, when the bare suspicion of having come from North of the Tweed, was a cause of hatred, contempt, and obloquy. The good nature and liberality of the English seem now even to have occasioned a re-action in their sentiments towards their neighbours, as if to atone for the national prejudices of their fathers. It becomes every Scotsman to acknowledge explicitly and with gratitude, that whatever tenable claim of merit has been made by his countrymen for more than twenty years back, whether in politics, arts, arms, professional distinction, or the paths of literature, it has been admitted by the English, not only freely, but with partial favour. The requital of North Britain can be little more than good wishes and sincere kindness towards her southern Sister, and a hospitable welcome to such of her children as are led by curiosity to visit Scotland. To this ought to be added the most grateful acknowledgment.

But though this amicable footing exists between the public of each nation, and such individuals of the other as may come into communication with them, and may God long continue it—yet, I must own, the conduct of England towards Scotland as a kingdom, whose crown was first united to theirs by our giving *them* a King, and whose dearest national rights were surrendered to them by an incorporating Union, has not been of late such as we were entitled to expect.

There has arisen gradually, on the part of England, a desire of engrossing the exclusive management of Scottish affairs, evinced by a number of circumstances, trifling in themselves, but forming a curious chain of proof when assembled together ; many of which intimate a purpose to abate us, like old Lear, of our train, and to accustom us to submit to petty slights and mortifications, too petty perhaps individually to afford subject of serious complaint, but which, while they tend to lower us in our own eyes, seem to lay the foundation for fresh usurpations, of which this meditated measure may be an example.

This difference of treatment, and of estimation, exhibited towards *individuals* of the Scottish nation, and to the *nation itself* as an aggregate, seems at first sight an inconsistency. Does a Scotchman approach London with some pretension to character as a Preacher, a Philosopher, a Poet, an Economist, or an Orator, he finds a welcome and all-hail, which sometimes surprises those whom he has left on the northern side of the Tweed,—little aware, perhaps, of the paragon who had emigrated, till they heard the acclamations attending his reception—Does a gentleman of private fortune take the same route, he finds a ready and voluntary admission into the class of society for which he is fitted by rank and condition—Is the visitor one of the numerous class who wander for the chance

of improving his fortunes, his national character
as a Scotsman is supposed to imply the desirable qualities of information, prudence, steadiness, moral and religious feeling, and he obtains
even a preference among the Southern employ-
ers, who want confidential clerks, land-stewards,
head-gardeners, or fit persons to occupy any
similar situation, in which the quality of trust-
worthiness is demanded.

But, on the other hand, if the English statesman has a point of great or lesser consequence
to settle with Scotland *as a country*, we find
him and his friends at once seized with a jealous, tenacious, wrangling, overbearing humour,
and that they not only insist upon conducting
the whole matter according to their own will,
but are by no means so accessible to the pleas
of reason, justice, and humanity, as might be
expected from persons in other cases so wise
and liberal. We cease at once to be the Northern Athenians, according to the slang of the
day—the moral and virtuous people, who are
practically and individually esteemed worthy of
especial confidence. We have become the cater-
pillars of the island, instead of its pillars. We

seem to be, in their opinion, once more trans-
muted into the Scots decribed by Churchill—a
sharp sharking race, whose wisdom is cunning,
and whose public spirit consists only in an illiberal nationality, inclining us, by every possible
exertion of craft, to obtain advantage at the expense of England.

Sir, the Englishman, just and liberal in his
ordinary and natural movements, is prone to feverish fits of suspicion, during which he is apt
to conceive that those qualities of frankness and
generosity render him peculiarly liable to be
imposed on. He will always *give* willingly, but
he often becomes shabby and litigious in making
a bargain. John Bull is in these points exactly
similar to his own Hotspur, who, in his dispute
with Glendower about the turning of the Trent,
exclaims,—

> " I do not care—I'll give thrice so much land
> To any well-deserving friend ;
> But in the way of *bargain*, mark ye me,
> I'll cavil on the ninth part of a hair."

The Continent has seen John in both these
moods ; and not being able to understand the
cause of the change, has been apt to suppose

L

his habits are entirely altered ; whereas they see only the same man in two different and extreme humours ; in one of which he would willingly relieve a begging vagabond, because the rascal must live ; and in the other, will hardly be brought to pay the bill of a poor tradesman, because he is afraid of being over-reached. The ancient and modern mode in which the English travellers did, and do now, pay their ordinary bills on the Continent, are an example of this piebald humour :—Formerly John travelled *en prince*, and even overlooked any species of imposition in innkeepers and *valets-de-place*, as not worth the care of *un homme tel que lui*. Now, he insists upon a preliminary contract— a solemn treaty for his *coutelet* and his *vin de pais*—and, neither for love of money, nor for want of money, but from a feverish apprehension that he may possibly be cheated in a reckoning, goes so miserably to work, that all the world cries " Shame on him !" *

To the better, more natural, more predomina-

---

* See the amusing work, called " The English in Italy."

ting disposition of our neighbours, I am well disposed to ascribe the many marks of partiality and kindness shown to individual Scotsmen by the English at large—to the latter suspicious, dogged, illiberal determination to have the best of the bargain,—that ungracious humour, which forgets even justice as well as liberal feelings, for fear their goodnature should be imposed upon,—I am compelled to ascribe much of their recent behaviour in international discussions. In such fits of jealousy, men are like those who wear green spectacles. Every object they look upon is tinged with the predominant colour, which exists not in the objects themselves, but in the medium through which they are viewed. Talk to an English statesman of the fairest, the most equitable proposal for the advancement of Scotland as a nation, the most just and indisputable claim on behalf of her public establishments or functionaries, the idea of a *Scotch Job* starts up like- an apparition, and frightens all power of equitable decision out of the Minister's head It is in vain urged, that even the expense of the proposed measure must be discharged by Scotland herself—her Sister is ready with the schoolboy's answer to his Fag,—" All that is *yours* is *ours*, and all *ours* is *our own*." Let the scales of Justice be trimmed with the nicest exactness if you will, but do not let Authority throw the sword into the scale from mere apprehension, lest, after having done her utmost to secure the advantage, she be cheated in the weighing.

In an old Scottish law, to be convicted of being an Egyptian, or gipsy, was equivalent to conviction that the party was a common and notorious thief. And truly the English seem to think, (in public matters, though by no means in private relations,) that being a Scotsman is equivalent to being an embezzler of public money, a jobber, and a peculator. But when they suppose that we are able and willing in all such cases to impose on them, they do injustice alike to their own shrewdness and our integrity.

It arises out of this unhappy state of feeling towards us, more than to any actual desire of giving us offence, that England has of late abated our establishment in many respects, in which our rank as a kingdom of the Union is in some degree compromised.

Last year a bill, deeply affecting the national

interests of Scotland, by altering many most important points in our judicature, was depending in Parliament. Grave objections appeared to the Law Bodies and others in Scotland, to attach to some particular arrangements thereby proposed. They required, not that the bill should be given up, but that it should be suspended at least, till the country in which it was to operate, and which alone was to be hurt or benefited by the enactment, should have time to consider the measure in all its bearings, and to express their national sense upon the subject. Can it be believed that it required the strongest possible remonstrances of the great Law-officer of the Crown with his Majesty's Ministers to obtain a few months' reprieve, as if the demolition, or alteration at least, of our laws, was a matter as little deserving a month's delay, as the execution of some flagrant criminal, justly and fully convicted of the most gross crimes? Take one or two instances more.

Till of late, there was generally an Admiral on this station; but since the gallant Sir John Beresford struck his flag, that mark of distinction seems to have been laid aside, probably for ever.

Our army establishment is dwindled to a shadow, scarce worthy of being placed under the command of the distinguished Major-General who now holds it, although he only commands the forces, instead of being, as was commonly the case till of late years, a Commander-in-Chief, with a Lieutenant-General, and two Major-Generals, under him. I need hardly say, that I would wish this abatement of our dignity, in some measure at least, amended, not by the *removal*, but by the *promotion* of the gallant General.

It may be replied that we are complimented in being thus left to ourselves—that we are a moral people, therefore do not require a military force to keep the peace—a loyal people, therefore do not need an armed force to put down tumult—that we have our own brave yeomanry, who, at no distant period, showed themselves capable of affording their country protection in the most desirable manner, anticipating mischief by their promptitude, and preventing evil before it had come to a head. But have these yeomen, who twice in a few months abandoned their homes at a few hours' warning, marched many miles, and by their demonstration of readiness, put an end to a very serious affair, and what might have been a very disastrous one—have they, I say, since that period, received the countenance due for their good will from the Government, and which should have been rendered alike in policy and justice? I am informed they have not. I am informed that they are, at least particular troops of them are, refused the small allowance made on the days when they are called out for exercise, and must either discharge the duty of training, always sufficiently expensive and inconvenient, entirely at their own expense, as some of them have done for two years, or suffer their discipline to fall into decay. Can it be that our English brethren have taken a notion that sabres are only curved broadswords, and that these are unhappy weapons in the hands of Scotsmen? I acquit them of such meanness. But they despise us a little too much.

Sir, Discontent is the child of Distress, and Distress is the daughter of ill-timed Experiment. Should we again see disorderly associations formed, and threats of open violence held out—should such a winter and spring as 1821

return, it may not, in the event of the measure
with which Scotland is threatened being inflicted on us, be quite so easy, as at that period, to
assemble on a given spot, within a day or two,
twelve or fourteen hundred yeomen to support
the handful of military left within Scotland.
That general spirit of loyalty will, I am sure,
be the same. But when proprietors are embar-
rassed, tenants distressed, commercial people in
doubt and danger, men lose at once their zeal,
and the means for serving the public. This is
not unworthy of serious consideration.

I mentioned in my former Letter another circumstance, of which I think my country has
reason to complain. It is that sort of absolute
and complete state of tutelage to which England seems disposed to reduce her sister country, subjecting her in all her relations to the
despotic authority of English Boards, which
exercise an exclusive jurisdiction in Scottish affairs, without regard to her local peculiarities,
and with something like contempt of her claims
as a country united with England, but which
certainly has never resigned the right of being
at least consulted in her own concerns. I men-

tioned the restrictions, and, as I conceive them, degrading incapacities, inflicted on our Revenue Boards,—I might extend the same observations to the regulations in the Stamp-Office ;—and I remember, when these were in progress, that it was said in good society, that the definitive instructions (verbal, I believe) communicated to the able officer upon whom the examination and adjustment of the alterations in that department devolved, and who was sent down hither on purpose, were to this purport :—" That he was to proceed in Scotland without more regard to the particular independence of that country than he would feel in Yorkshire." These, however, were matters interesting the general revenue—the servants of the Crown had a right to regulate them as they pleased. But if they were regulated with a purposed and obvious intention to lessen the consequence of Scotland, throw implied discredit on her natives, as men unworthy of trust, and hold her recollections and her feelings at nought, they make links in a chain which seems ready to be wound around us whenever our patience will permit.

This, sir, is an unwise, nay, an unsafe pro-

ceeding. An old chain, long worn, forms a cal-
losity on the limb which bears it, and is endured,
with whatever inconvenience, as a thing of custom. It is not so with restraints newly imposed.
These fret—gall—gangrene—the iron enters
first into the flesh, and then into the soul. I
speak out what more prudent men would keep
silent. I may lose friends by doing so ; but he
who is like Malachi Malagrowther, old and un-
fortunate, has not many to lose, and risks little
in telling truths before, when men of rising am-
bition and budding hopes would leave them to
be discovered by the event. The old tree and
the withered leaf are easily parted.

But, besides such matters of punctilio, Mr
Journalist, there has been in England a gradual
and progressive system of assuming the management of affairs entirely and exclusively proper
to Scotland, as if we were totally unworthy of
having the management of our own concerns.
All must centre in London. We could not have
a Caledonian Canal, but the Commissioners must
be Englishmen, and meet in London ;—a most
useful canal they would have made of it, had
not the lucky introduction of steam-boats—
—*Deus ex machina*—come just in time to re-

deem them from having made the most expensive and most useless undertaking of the kind ever heard of since Noah floated his ark ! We could not be intrusted with the charge of erecting our own kirks, (churches in the Highlands,) or of making our roads and bridges in the same wild districts, but these labours must be conducted under the tender care of men who knew nothing of our country, its wants and its capabilities, but who, nevertheless, sitting in their office in London, were to decide, without appeal, upon the conduct of the roads in Lochaber !— Good Heaven, sir ! to what are we fallen ?—or rather, what are we esteemed by the English ? Wretched drivellers, incapable of understanding our own affairs ; or greedy peculators, unfit to be trusted ? On what ground are we considered either as the one or the other ?

But I may perhaps be answered, that these operations are carried on by grants of public money ; and that, therefore, the English—undoubtedly the only disinterested and public-spirited and trust-worthy persons in the universe—must be empowered exclusively to look after its application. Public money forsooth !!!

I should like to know whose pocket it comes out of. Scotland, I have always heard, contributes FOUR MILLIONS to the public revenue. I should like to know, before we are twitted with grants of public money, how much of that income is dedicated to Scottish purposes—how much applied to the general uses of the empire—and if the balance should be found to a great amount on the side of Scotland, as I suspect it will, I should like still farther to know how the English are entitled to assume the direction and disposal of any pittance which may be permitted, out of the produce of our own burthens, to revert to the peculiar use of the nation from which it has been derived ? If England was giving us alms, she would have a right to look after the administration of them, lest they should be misapplied or embezzled. If she is only consenting to afford us a small share of the revenue derived from our own kingdom, we have some title, methinks, to be consulted in the management, nay, intrusted with it.

This assumption of uncalled-for guardianship accelerates the circulation a little, and inclines one to say to his countrymen,

Our blood has been too cold and temperate,
Unapt to stir at such indignities———.

You could not keep a decent servant in your family, sir, far more a partner, if you obviously treated such a person as a man in whom no confidence was to be reposed even in his own department. A ludicrous mode has been lately fallen upon of keeping up in appearance, and, as far as the almanack goes, our old list of Scottish offices. First, they deprive a high office of state of all its emoluments, and then they unite it with one to which some emolument is still permitted to attach ; so they are doubled, like slices of bread and butter laid face to face—English fashion, as schoolboys used to call it—with this great difference that only one slice is buttered—an improvement which would scarce suit John Bull's taste. The office of Lord Clerk Register is thus united with that of the Keeper of the Signet, with the emolument attached to the last alone.* It was at another time proposed, on

---

* The Right Hon. Lord Clerk Register has deserved what he will think better than either office or salary—the solemn thanks of his countrymen, for the frank and decided tone which he has taken in the Currency Question.

the same liberal footing, to unite the office of
the Lord Justice-General, (salary suppressed,)
though I believe the bill did not pass.

This is really, sir, putting the few offices we
have left to indicate our ancient independence,
on a more ridiculous footing than the Dukes of
Normandy and Acquitaine, which imaginary
vassals of England used to revive at every co-
ronation, and were each of them allowed a whole
man to represent them ;* while poor Scotland's
high officers of state resemble Coleman's

> Two single gentlemen roll'd into one ;

or rather remind us of the starvling shifts of
a strolling company, in which two parts are
performed by one actor, and for one salary.
There may be an emblem in the thing though.
It is perhaps designed to represent an union
between two kingdoms, or an incorporating
union, in which one enjoys the full advantages and supereminent authority, and the other
remains,

---

* The good taste which directed the last august ceremony,
dispensed with the appearance of these phantoms.

Magni nominis umbra.

I do not suppose this farce will be continued long. We shall in due time, I suppose, be put all under English control, deprived even of the few native dignitaries and office-holders we have left, and accommodated with a set of English superintendants in every department. It will be upon the very reasoning of Goneril before alluded to :—

> " What need you five-and-twenty, ten, or five,
> To follow in a house where twice so many
> Have a command to tend you ?—"

Patrick, will you play Regan, and echo,

> "——What need *one* ?"

Take care, my good fellow ! for you will scarce get a great share in our spoils, and will be shortly incapacitated, and put under a statute of lunacy, as well as ourselves.

But what will England take by this engrossing spirit ? Not the miserable candle-ends and cheese-parings—these, I dare say, she scorns. The mere pleasure, then, of absolute authority —the gratification of humour exacted by a peevish and petted child, who will not be contented till he has the toy in his own hand, though he break it the next moment. Is any real power derived by centering the immediate and direct control of everything in London? Far from it. On the contrary, that great metropolis is already a head too bulky for the empire, and, should it take a vertigo, the limbs would be unable to support it. The misfortune of France, during the Revolution, in all its phases, was, that no part of the kingdom could think for itself or act for itself; all were from habit necessitated to look up to Paris. Whoever was uppermost there, and the worst party is apt to prevail in a corrupted metropolis, were, without possibility of effectual contradiction, the uncontrolled and despotic rulers of France—*absit omen!*

Again, would the British empire become stronger, were it possible to annul and dissolve all the distinctions and peculiarities, which, flowing out of circumstances, historical events, and difference of customs and climates, make its relative parts still, in some respects, three separate nations, though intimately incorporated into one empire?

Every rope-maker knows, sir, that three distinct *strands*, as they are called, incorporated and twisted together, will make a cable ten times stronger than the same quantity of hemp, however artificially combined into a single twist of cord. The reason is obvious to the meanest capacity. If one of the strands happen to fail a little, there is a threefold chance that no imperfection will occur in the others at the same place, so that the infirm strand may give way a little, yet the whole cord remain trustworthy. If the single twist fail at any point, all is over. For God's sake, sir, let us remain as Nature made us, Englishmen, Irishmen, and Scotchmen, with something like the impress of our several countries upon each! We would not become better subjects, or more valuable members of the common empire, if we all resembled each other like so many smooth shillings. Let us love and cherish each other's virtues—bear with each other's failings—be tender to each other's prejudices—be scrupulously regardful of each other's rights. Lastly, let us borrow each other's improvements, but never before they are needed and demanded. The degree of national diversity between dif-

M

ferent countries, is but an instance of that general variety which Nature seems to have
adopted as a principle through all her works, as
anxious, apparently, to avoid, as modern statesmen to enforce, anything like an approach to
absolute " uniformity."

It may be said that some of the grievances I
have complained of are mere trifles. I grant
they are,—excepting in the feelings and intentions towards Scotland which they indicate.
But, according to Bacon's maxim, you will see
how the wind sits by flinging up a feather,
which you cannot discern by throwing up a
stone. Affronts are almost always more offensive than injuries, although they seldom are in
themselves more than trifles. The omitting to
discharge a gun or two in a salute, the raising
or striking of a banner or sail, have been the
source of bloody wars. England lost America
about a few miserable chests of tea—she endan-
gered India for the clipping of a mustachio.

But let us humble ourselves to our situation,
and confine our remonstrances to the immediate
grievance, which surely cannot be termed punc-
tilious or unimportant.

To England we say, therefore, Let us appeal
from Philip intoxicated to Philip sober. Leave
out exasperating circumstances on either side,
and examine our remonstrance, not in the jealous feeling of which we have reason to complain, but in the gentlemanlike and liberal
tone so much more becoming a great nation,
and according, I must say, so much better with
your natural disposition. As you mean that
a value should be set upon your free public
voice by your legislators, allow the natural influence of that of Scotland, in a matter exclusively relating to her own affairs, but so intimately connected with her welfare, that nothing
since the year 1748 has occurred of such importance. The precedent is a bad one at any
rate ; the consequences will be much worse.

> Prevent—resist it. Let it not be so,
> Lest children's children call against you—*woe!*

Our Scottish Nobles and Gentlemen, I cannot
better exhort to resist the proposal at every
stage, by the most continued and unremitting
opposition—to be discouraged by nothing—to
hope to the last—to combat to the last—than
by using once more the words of the patriotic

Belhaven :—" Man's extremity is God's opportunity. He is a present help in time of need ; a deliverer, and that right early. Some unforeseen providence will fall out, that may cast the balance. Some Joseph will say, Why do you strive together when you are brethren ? Some Judah or other will say, Let not our hand be upon him, he is our brother. Let us up then, and be doing ; and let our noble patriots behave themselves like men, and we know not how soon a blessing may come."

I am, Mr Journalist,

Yours,

MALACHI MALAGROWTHER.

EDINBURGH :
Printed by James Ballantyne and Co.

A

THIRD LETTER

TO THE

Editor of the Edinburgh Weekly Journal,

FROM

MALACHI MALAGROWTHER, Esq.

ON THE

PROPOSED CHANGE OF CURRENCY,

AND

OTHER LATE ALTERATIONS,

AS THEY AFFECT, OR ARE INTENDED TO AFFECT,

THE

KINGDOM OF SCOTLAND.

Macduff. Stands Scotland where it did ?
Rosse. Alas ! poor country.

THIRD EDITION.

EDINBURGH :

Printed by James Ballantyne and Company,

FOR WILLIAM BLACKWOOD, EDINBURGH : AND

T. CADELL, STRAND, LONDON.

1826.

LETTER THIRD

ON THE

PROPOSED CHANGE OF CURRENCY.

TO THE EDITOR

OF THE EDINBURGH WEEKLY JOURNAL.

DEAR MR JOURNALIST,

THIS third set of Mr Baxter's last words is rather a trial on your patience, considering how much *Balaam* (speaking technically) I have edged out of your valuable paper; how I have trodden on the toes of your Domestic Intelligence, and pushed up to the wall even your Political Debates, until you have almost lost your honoured title of the EDINBURGH JOURNAL in that of MALACHI'S CHRONICLE.

I returned from the Meeting of Inhabitants on Friday last, sir, convoked for considering

this question, with much feeling of gratification
from what I saw and heard; but still a little
disappointed that no one appeared on the opposite side, excepting one gentleman, ("self pull-
ing," as Captain Crowe says, " against the whole
ship's crew,") whose eloquence used no other
argument than by recommending implicit deference to the wisdom of Ministers. I am a
pretty stanch Tory myself, but not up to this
point of humility. I never have nor will bargain for an implicit surrender of my private
judgement in a national question of this sort. I
am but an unit, but of units the whole sum of
society is composed. On the present question,
had I been the born servant of Ministers, I
would have used to them the words of Cornwall's dependant, when he interferes to prevent
his master from treading out Gloster's eyes—

> I have served you ever since I have been a child,
> But better service have I never done you,
> Than now to bid you *Hold*.

Or in a yet more spirited passage in the same
drama—

> ———— Be Kent unmannerly.
> When Lear is mad.

To return to the business. By the unanimity of the meeting, I lost an opportunity of making a very smart extempore speech, which I had sate up half the night for the purpose of composing. To have so much eloquence die within me unuttered, excited feelings like those of Sancho, when, in the deserts of the Sierra Morena, his good things rotted in his gizzard. To console me, however, I found, on my return to my lodgings in the Lawn-market, my own lucubrations blazing in the goodly form of two responsible pamphlets. I seized on them as if I had never seen them before, and recited the more animated passages aloud, striding up and down a room, in which, from its dimensions, striding is not very convenient. I ended with reading aloud the motto, which I designed in the pride of my heart to prefix to my immortal twins, when, side by side, under the same comely cover, they shall travel down to posterity as a crown octavo ;—

> He set a bugle to his mouth,
>   And blew a blast sae shrill,
> The trees in greenwood shook thereat,
>   Sae loud rang ilka hill.

But while I mentally claimed for myself the honour of alarming Scotland, from Coldstream Bridge to the far Highlands, I was giving, by the noise I made, far greater alarm to my neighbour, Christopher Chrysal, who keeps the small hardware and miscellaneous shop under the turnpike stair. Now, sir, you must know that Chrysal deals occasionally in broken tea-spoons and stray sugar-tongs, dismantled lockets and necklaces, (which have passed with more or less formality from ladies to their waiting-maids,) seals, out of which valets have knocked the stones that the setting might be rendered avail-able, and such other small gear,—nay, I once saw an old silver coffee-pot in his possession. On the score, therefore, of being connected with the precious metals by his calling, neighbour Chrysal has set himself up for a patron and pro-tector of Gold and Silver, and a stout contender for Bullion currency. With a half-crown in one hand, and a twenty-shilling note in the other, he will spout like a player over the two pictures in Hamlet, and it is great to hear him address them alternately—

THIS is the thing itself—Off, off, ye lendings!

But with all the contempt he expressed for the paper substitute, I have always seen that it steals quietly back to the solitude of his little pocket-book. Indeed, the barber says Mr Chrysal has other reasons for wishing a change of currency, or a currency of change, in respect of his own acceptances not being in these sharp times quite so locomotive as usual—They love the desk of the holder, sir, better than the counter of his great Neighbours in Bank Street. You understand me—but I hate scandal.

I had no sooner apologized to Christopher for the disturbance I had occasioned, (which I did with some shame of countenance,) than I politely offered him a copy of my pamphlet. He thanked me, but added with a grin, (for you know no man is a prophet in his own common stair,) that he had nothing particular to wrap up at present : " But in troth, Mr Malachi," said he, " I looked over your pamphlet in the reading-room, and I must tell you as a friend, you have just made a fool of yourself, Mr Malachi." " A fool !" replied I ; " when, how, and in what manner ?" " Ye have set out, sir," replied he,—for Chrysal is a kind of orator, and

speaks as scholarly and wisely as his neighbours,
—" with assuming the principle, which you
should have proved.—You say, that in consequence of restoring the healthful currency of the
precious metals, instead of keeping those ragged
scraps of paper, Scotland will experience a want
of the circulating medium, by which deprivation
her industry will be cramped, her manufactures
depressed, her fisheries destroyed, and so forth.
But you know nothing of the nature of the precious metals, and how should you ?"

" Why, not by dealing in old thimbles, broken buckles, and children's whistles, certainly, or
stolen *sprecherie*," said I ; " but speak out, man,
wherein do I evince ignorance of the nature of
the precious metals—tell me that ?"

" Why, Mr Malachi Malagrowther," said my
friend, in wrath, " I pronounce you ignorant of
the most ordinary principles of Political Economy. In your unadvised tract there, you have
shown yourself as irritable as Balaam, and as obstinate as his ass. You are making yourself and
other people fidgetty about the want of gold, to
supply the place of that snuff-paper of yours ;
now in this I repeat you are ignorant."

Here he raised his voice, as if speaking *ex cathedra*. " Gold," continued he, " is a commodity itself, though it be also the representative of other commodities ; just as a Banker is a man, though his business is to deal in money. Gold, therefore, like all other commodities, will flow to the place where there is a demand for it. It will be found, assure yourself, wherever it is most wanted ; just as, if you dig a well, water will percolate into it from all the neighbourhood. Twenty years ago you could not have seen a cigar in Edinburgh. Gillespie, the greatest snuff-merchant of his day, would not have known what you wanted had you asked him for one ; and now the shop-windows of the dealers are full of real Havannahs,—and why ?—because you see every writer's apprentice with a cigar in his mouth. It is the demand that makes the supply, and so it will be with the gold. The balance of free-trade, whether the commodity be gold or grain, will go where the one finds mouths to be fed, the other a currency to be supported. What sent specie into the lagoons of Venice, and into the swamps of Holland formerly, as well as into the emporium of London now, while large cities, situated under a finer climate, and in a more fertile country, were and are comparatively destitute of the precious metals?—what, save the tendency of commerce, like water, to find its own just level, and to send all the commodities subject to its influence, the precious metals included, to the points where they are most wanted ?"

Now, Mr Journalist, I am a man of a quick temper, but somewhat of a slow wit ; and though it struck me that there was something fallacious in this argument, yet, bolstered out as it was by his favourite metaphor, it sounded so plausible, that the right answer did not at once occur to me. Chrysal went on in triumph : " You speak of your Fisheries and Kelp manufacture, and such like, and seem to dread that they will be all ruined for want of a circulating medium. But, sir, one of two things must happen. Either, FIRST, assuming that these branches of industry are beneficial to the individuals, and make advantageous returns ; as such they will have the usual power of attracting towards them the specie necessary to carry them on, and of course no change whatever will take place. Or, SE-

CONDLY, these fisheries, and so forth, produce
no adequate return for the labour expended on
them, and are therefore a compulsory species of
manufacture, like those establishments institu-
ted at the direct expense, and under the immediate control of government, which we see fading
in despotic countries, or only deriving a sickly
existence by the expenditure of the Sovereign,
and not by their own natural vigour. In that
latter case," he pursued, "those fishing and
kelping operations are not productive—are useless to the country—and ought not to be carried on an hour longer; they only occasion the
mis-employment of so much capital, the loss
of so much labour. Leave your kelp-rocks to
the undisturbed possession of seals and mer-
maids, if there be any—you will buy *barilla*
cheaper in South America. Send your Highland fishers to America and Botany Bay, where
they will find plenty of food, and let them leave
their present sterile residence in the utter and
undisturbed solitude for which Nature designed
it. Do not think you do any hardship in obeying the universal law of nature, which leads
wants and supplies to draw to their just and

proper level, and equalize each other; which attracts gold to those spots, and those only, where it can be profitably employed, and induces man to transport himself from the realms of famine to those happier regions, where labour is light and subsistence plentiful.

"Lastly," said the unconscionable Christopher, "sweep out of your head, Mr Malachi, all that absurd rubbish of ancient tradition and history about national privileges—you might as well be angry with the Provost who pulled down the Lucken-booths. They do not belong to this day, in which so many changes have taken place, and so many more are to be expected. We look for what is USEFUL, sir, and to what is useful only; and our march towards utility is not to be interrupted by reference to antiquated treaties, or obsolete prejudices. So, while you sit flourishing your claymore, Mr Malachi, on the top of your Articles of Union, very like the figure of a Highlander on the sign of a whisky-office, take care you are not served as the giant who built his castle on the marvellous bean-stalk— Truth comes like the old woman with the 'cuttie-axe'—it costs but a swashing blow or two,

and down comes Malachi and his whole system."
—So saying, *exit* Christopher, *ovans*.

There was such a boldness and plausibility
about the fellow, and such a confidence in the
arguments which he expressed so fluently, that
I felt a temporary confusion of ideas, and was
obliged to throw myself into what has been, for
many generations, the considering position of
the Malagrowther family : that is to say, I flung
myself back in our hereditary easy-chair, fixing
my eyes on the roof, but keeping them, at the
same time, half shut ; having my hands folded,
and twirling my thumbs slowly around each
other, a motion highly useful in unravelling and
evolving the somewhat tangled thread of the
ideas. Thus seated, in something short of two
hours I succeeded in clearing out the ravelled
skean, which evolved itself in as orderly a coil
before me as if it had been touched by the rod
of Prince Percinet, in the fairy tale, and I am
about to communicate the result. I must needs
own that my discoveries went so far as was like
to have involved you in an examination of the
general principles on which the doctrine of currency depends. But since, *entre nous*, we might

N

get a little beyond our depth on the subject, I have restrained myself within the limits of the question, as practically applicable to Scotland.

My present business is to inquire how this meditated change of circulation, supposing it forcibly imposed on us, is to be accomplished— by what magic art, in other words, our paper is to be changed into gold, without some great national distress, nay, convulsion, *in transitu*?

My neighbour deems anxiety in this case quite ridiculous. Gold, he says, is a commodity, and whenever its presence becomes necessary, there it will appear. Guineas, according to Christopher, are like the fairy goblets in Parnell's tale,

——that with a wish come nigh,
And with a wish retire.

I don't know how it may be in national necessities, but I have some reason to think that friend Chrysal has not, any more than I have myself, found the maxim true, in so far as concerns our personal experience. I heartily wish, indeed, this comfortable doctrine extended to individual cases, and that the greater occasion a poor devil had for money, the more certain he should be of his wants being supplied by the arrival of that obliging article, which is said to come wherever it is wanted. Since Fortunatus's time, the contrary has in general proved to be the case, and I cannot deny it would be very convenient to us to have his system restored.

And yet there is some truth in what my neighbour says ; for if a man is indispensably obliged to have a sum of money, why he must make every effort to raise it. Supposing I was in business, and threatened with insolvency, I might find myself under the necessity of getting cash by selling property at an under rate, or procuring loans at usurious interest on what I retained, and in that ruinous manner I might raise money, because still nearer ruin stared me in the face if I did not. The question is, how long supplies so obtained could continue ?—Not an instant longer than I have articles to sell or to pawn. After this, my usual wants would be as pressing, but I might wish my heart out ere I found a groat to relieve them—No fairy will leave a silver penny in my shoe. Now I fear it must be by some such violent sacrifices, as those in the case supposed, that Scotland must purchase and maintain her metallic currency, if her present substitute is debarred.

Mr Chrysal's proposition should not then run, that gold will come when it is most needed, but should have been expressed thus,—that in countries where the presence of gold is rendered indispensable, it must be obtained, whatever price is given for it, while the means of paying such a price remain.

He amuses himself, indeed, and puzzles his hearers, by affirming that gold is like water, and, like water when poured out, it will find its level.—A metaphor is no argument in any instance ; but I think I can contrive in the present to turn my friend's own water-engine against him. Scotland, sir, is not *beneath* the level to which gold flows naturally. She is *above* that level, and she may perish for want of it ere she sees a guinea, without she, or the State for her, be at the perpetual expense of maintaining, by constant expenditure of a large per centage, that metallic currency which has a natural tendency to escape from a poor country back to a rich one. Just so, a man might die of thirst on the top of a Scottish hill, though a river or a lake lay at the base of it. Therefore, if we insist upon the favourite comparison of gold to water, we must conceive the possibility of the golden Pactolus flowing up Glencroe in an opposite direction to the natural element, which trots down from the celebrated *Rest and be Thankful.*

If my friend would consult the clerk of the Water Company, at his office in the Royal Exchange, he would explain the matter at once. " Let me have," says Mr Chrysal, " a pipe of water to my house."—" Certainly, sir ; it will cost you forty shillings yearly."—" The devil it will ! Why, surely the Lawnmarket is lower than the Reservoir on the Castlehill ? It is the nature of water to come to a level. What title have you to charge me money, when the element is only obeying the laws of Nature, and descending to its level ?"—" Very true, sir," replies the clerk ; " but then it was no law of Nature brought it to the reservoir, at a height which was necessary to enable us to disperse the supply over the city. On the contrary, it was an exertion of Art in despite of Nature. It was forced hither by much labour and ingenuity. Lakes were formed, aqueducts constructed,

rivers dammed up, pipes laid for many miles.
Without immense expense, the water could never have been brought here ; and without your
paying a rateable charge, you cannot have the
benefit of it."

This is exactly the case with the gold currency. It must have a natural tendency to
centre in London, for the exchange is heavily
against Scotland. We have the whole public income, four millions a-year, to remit thither. Independent of that large and copious drain, we
have occasion to send to England the rents of
non-resident proprietors, and a thousand other
payments to make to London, which must be
done in specie, or by bills payable in the metropolis.   So that the circulation moves thither of
free will, like a horse led by the bridle ; while
Scotland's attempts to detain it, are like those of
a wild Highlandman catching his pony by the
tail. Or, to take a very old comparison, London
is like Aboulcasem's well, full of gold, gems, and
everything valuable.   The rich contents are
drawn from it by operations resembling those
of a forcing-pump, which compel small portions
into the extreme corners of the kingdom ; but

all these golden streamlets, when left to themselves, trickle back to the main reservoir.

My friend's idea of a voluntary, unsolicited, and unbought supply of metallic currency, is like the reasoning of old Merrythought, when, with only a shilling in his pocket, he expresses a resolution to continue a jovial course of life. " But how wilt thou come by the means, Charles ?" says his wife. " How ?" replied the gay old gentleman, in a full reliance on his resources,—" How ?—Why, how have I done hitherto, these forty years ?—I never came into my dining-room, but, at eleven and six o'clock, I found excellent meat and drink on the table. My clothes were never worn out, but next morning a tailor brought me a new suit, and, without question, it will be so ever—use makes perfectness." The dramatist has rescued his jolly epicurean out of the scrape before his slender stock was exhausted ; but in what mode Scotland is to be relieved from the expense about to be imposed on a country, where industry and skill can but play a saving game, at best, against national disadvantages, is not so easy to imagine.

What may be the expense of purchasing in the outset, and maintaining in constant supply, a million and a half of gold, I cannot pretend to calculate, but something may be guessed from the following items :—To begin, like Mrs Glass's recipe for dressing a hare, *first catch your hare* —first buy your gold at whatever sacrifice of loss of exchange ; then add to the price a reasonable profit to those who are to advance the purchase-money—next insure your specie against water-thieves and land-thieves, peril of winds, waves, and rocks, from the Mint to the wharf, from the wharf to Leith, from Leith to Edinburgh, from Edinburgh to the most remote parts of Scotland, unprotected by police of any kind—the insurances can be no trifle ; besides, that an accident or two, like the loss of the Delight smack the other day, with L.4000 of specie on board, will make a tolerably heavy addition to other bills of charges, as the expense of carriages, guards, and so forth—then add the items together, and compute the dead loss of interest upon the whole sum. The whole may be moderately calculated at an expense of more than *five per cent*, a charge which must ultimately be laid on the Scottish manufactures, agricultural operations, fisheries, and other public and private undertakings ; many of which are not at present returning twelve or fifteen per cent of profit at the uttermost.

My friend Chrysal's reasoning rested on this great mistake, that he confounds the necessity of our procuring gold under the operation of the new system, and the supplies which that necessity must necessarily oblige us to purchase, with a voluntary determination of unbought treasures running up-hill to find their level at Stornoway, Tongue, or Oban. He imagines that the specie, for which we have to pay a heavy consideration, will come to our service voluntarily. I answer, in one word, the gold will come, if purchased, AND NOT OTHERWISE. The expense attending the operation will be just a tax upon the parties who pay it, with this difference, that it makes no addition to the public revenue. Every sovereign we get, which passes of course for twenty shillings, will, before it gets to the north of Scotland, have cost *one*-and-twenty. Illustrations of so plain a proposition are endless. Suppose Government had imposed a stamp-duty upon any commodity, and, whilst with some other cowl'd neighbours I am canvassing its effects, I ask, as a party concerned,—" But how are we to come by these stamps? The branch of commerce to which they apply is not able to bear the impost." Up rises my friend Chrysal in reply—" Stamped paper," says he, " is a commodity; and, like all commodities, flows to the point where there is a demand." True—but, unhappily, when the stamp-paper is in bodily presence, I cannot have a slip of it till I pay the impost; and if my trade does not enable me to do so, I must give it up, or be a ruined man!

The same consequences must attend the increased expense of the circulation under the proposed measure, as would apply to a tax in any other form. The manufactures, public works, and private speculations, which are making a return, enabling them to defray the charge attending the more expensive medium of circulation, will struggle on as they can, with less profit by the direct amount, and more disadvantages arising from the means of circulation being at the mercy of winds and waves, and subjected to long and perilous transportation before the gold reaches them. Those, on the other hand, whose trade makes more precarious returns, will be no longer able to wait for better times. They will give up all, and the consequences to Scotland—and England also—omitting all allusion to individual distress, will be a black history.

I have already said, that the Fisheries and Kelp shores, and improvements on the more bleak and distant districts, will probably be the first sufferers. And my neighbour replies, with a sweeping argument, that enterprises which cannot support themselves by their own exertions, and natural returns of profit, ought not to have the encouragement of Government— that they are only vain schemes, in which labour and expense are wasted without their bringing the necessary return, and that the force employed in keeping up these barren and fruitless undertakings should, as soon as possible, be directed into a more productive channel. If I urge, that, although these undertakings may not, as yet, have made the full returns expected, yet they support many people, natives of a country otherwise too poor to furnish the means of livelihood to its inhabitants,—why, the answer is equally ready. Let the Highlander emigrate, or be transported to Botany Bay; and supply his place with sheep,—goats, —anything,—or nothing at all.

I do not mean to deny, sir, that there is general truth in the maxims, which recommend that a free trade be left to sustain itself by its own exertions; deprecating the system of forcing commerce when its natural efforts were not successful, and warning against planting colonies in unhealthy or barren spots, where the colonists must perish, or exist in a state of miserable and precarious dependence on the bounties of the mother country. To these political truths I subscribe cheerfully.—But an old civilian used to tell me, *fraus latet in generalibus;* and no general maxim can be safely, wisely, or justly applied, until it has been carefully considered how far it is controlled by the peculiar circumstances of the case. The precepts of Religion herself, as expressed in the holiest texts of Scripture, have been wrested into sophistry—the soundest political principles may, by the frigid subtleties of metaphysical moonshine, be extended so as, in appearance, to authorise aggressions on national rights, as well

as on the dictates of sound wisdom and humanity.

I have more replies than one to my neighbour's doctrines of Political Economy, (though
true in the abstract,) when I consider them as
applicable to the case in question.

In the *first* place, I deny that the Scottish
Fisheries are in the predicament to which the
maxim, quoted triumphantly by my friend
Chrysal, applies. I say that they are already
supporting themselves, and producing a moderate but certain profit; only that this profit is
as yet *so* moderate, that it certainly will not
bear an impost of probably five or six per cent
upon the gross capital employed ; and that,
therefore, it is the highest impolicy to smother,
by such a burthen, important national undertakings, which are, without such new imposition, in a condition to maintain themselves. It
would be breaking the reed ere it had attained
its strength, and quenching the smoking flax
just when about to burst into flame.

Secondly, Admitting, from the great poverty
of the inhabitants, and other discouraging circumstances, that the Scottish fisheries have for

a long time required the support of Government, I still aver, that the expense attending such support has been well and wisely disposed of,—just as a landlord would act not generously only, but most prudently, in giving favourable terms of settlement to a tenant, who was to improve his farm largely. An exotic shrub, when first planted, must be watered and cared for—a child requires tenderness and indulgence till he has got through the sickly and helpless years of infancy. A fishery or manufacture, established in a wild country, and among a population of indolent habits, unaccustomed to industry, and to the enjoyment of the profits derived from it, will at the outset require assistance from the State, till old habits are surmounted, and difficulties overcome. There is something in the nature of the people, who have been long depressed by poverty, resembling the qualities of their own peat-earth. Left alone, it is the most anti-septic and inert of Nature's productions; but when, according to the process of compost invented by the late ingenious Lord Meadowbank, this *caput mortuum* is intermixed with a small portion of active manure, it heats.

ferments, changes its sluggish nature, and fertilizes the whole country in the vicinity. No agriculturist regards the expense of the proportion of manure necessary to commence this vivifying operation ; and neither will any wise government regret the outlay of sums employed in exciting the industry, improving the comforts, and amending the condition, of its inhabitants. In the present case, Government has done this duty amply—The tree has taken root, the child is rising fast to youth and manhood— the establishments of the fisheries are in full progress to triumphant success. The question is not, if you are yet to continue your encouragement—nor whether the public is to save some expense by withdrawing it. In these questions there would be a direct and palpable motive, that of a saving to the State, which, so far as it went, would be a real, if not an adequate motive, for breaking up these establishments. But the question at issue turns on this very different point—whether, by a measure obnoxious to Scotland, and in which England cannot challenge an interest remote or direct, you are to adopt an enactment so likely to

create the ruin of these establishments, now
that they have already attained prosperity?
The wish of many of the wisest English patriots has been accomplished—the barren and
desolate shores are compensated in that desola-
tion by the riches of the sea—foreigners are
driven from engrossing as formerly their wealth,
and selling to Britain herself, at advantage, the
produce of her own coasts. Thriving villages
are already found where there were scarcely to
be seen the most wretched hovels ; a population
lazy and indolent, because they had no motive
for exertion, have become, on finding the employment, and tasting the fruits of industry,
an enterprizing and hardy race of seamen, well
qualified to enrich their country in peace—to
defend her in time of war. *All this* is GAIN-
ED. Shall all be lost again, to render the system of currency betwixt England and Scotland uniform ? all sacrificed to what I can call
little more than a political conundrum ? In my
opinion, the Dutchmen might as well cut the
dikes, and let the sea in upon the land their industry has gained from it. In the case of Holland, she would at least save the money ex-

pended in maintaining her ramparts. In our case, the state gains nothing and loses everything.

Lastly, I would say a word in behalf of the people of Scotland, merely as human beings, and entitled to consideration as such. I will suppose this alteration is recommended by some expected advantages of great importance, but the nature of which are prudently concealed. I will suppose, what is not easily understood, that in some unintelligible manner England is to gain with addition what Scotland is condemned to lose. (The process, by the way, seems to resemble that recommended by Moliere's quack, who prescribes the putting out of one eye, that the other may see further, and more acutely.) I will suppose that our statesmen, by enforcing this measure, condemn to emigration, or transportation —the punishment she inflicts on felons—the inhabitants of distant and desert tracts, on the mainland and in the Hebrides, to save her from some expense, and because she thinks a country so different from her own fertile valleys, cannot be fit for human habitation. In that case, I would say, Consider, first, the character of the

O

population you are about to consign thus summarily to the effects which must follow the destroying their present means of livelihood. My countrymen have their faults, and I am well aware of them. But this I will say, that there is more vice, more crime—nay, more real want and misery, more degrading pauperism and irremediable wretchedness, in the parish of Saint Giles's alone, than in the whole Highlands and pastoral districts of Scotland, or perhaps in all Scotland together. Poor as the inhabitants are, the wants of the Highlanders are limited to their circumstances ; and they have enjoyments which make amends, in their own way of reckoning, for deprivations which they do not greatly feel. Their land is to them a land of many recollections. I will not dwell on that subject, lest I be thought fantastic in harping on a tune so obsolete. But every heart must feel some sympathy when I say, they love their country, rude as it is, because it holds the churches where their fathers worshipped, and the churchyards where their bones are laid.

This is not all. Mountainous countries inspire peculiarly strong attachments into the natives, showing perhaps, if we argue up to the Final Great Cause, that while it was the pleasure of God that men should exist in all parts of the world, which His pleasure called into being, the Beneficence of the Common Father annexed circumstances of consolation, which should compensate the mountaineers for want of the fertility and fine climate enjoyed by the inhabitants of the plain. Some philosophers, looking to secondary causes, have referred the sense of this local attachment amongst mountaineers to the influence of the sublime though desolate scenery around them, as stamping the idea of a peculiar country more deeply on their bosoms. The chief cause seems to me to be, that such tribes rarely change their dwellings, and therefore become more wedded to their native districts than are the inhabitants of those where the population is frequently fluctuating. The land is not only theirs *now*, it pertained to a long list of fathers before them ; and the coldest philosopher will regard what is called a family estate with greater attachment than he applies to a recent purchase.

But independent of this, the inhabitants of

the wilder districts in Scotland have actually
some enjoyments, both moral and physical,
which compensate for the want of better subsistence and more comfortable lodging. In a word,
they have more liberty than the inhabitants of
the richer soil. Englishmen will start at this as
a paradox; but it is very true notwithstanding, that if one great privilege of liberty be the
power of going where a man pleases, the Scotch
peasant enjoys it much more than the English.
The pleasure of viewing " fair Nature's face,"
and a great many other primitive enjoyments,
for which a better diet and lodging are but
indifferent substitutes, are more within the
power of the poor man in Scotland than in the
sister country. A Scottish gentleman, in the
wilder districts, is seldom severe in excluding
his poor neighbours from his grounds; and I
have known many that have voluntarily thrown
them open to all quiet and decent persons who
wish to enjoy them. The game of such liberal
proprietors, their plantations, their fences, and
all that is apt to suffer from intruders, have, I
have observed, been better protected than where

severer measures of general seclusion were adopted. *Haud inexpertus loquor.*

But in many districts, the part of the soil which, with the utmost stretch of appropriation, the first-born of Egypt can set apart for his own exclusive use, bears a small proportion indeed to the uncultivated wastes. The step of the mountaineer on his wild heath, solitary mountain, and beside his far-spread lake, is more free than that which is confined to a dusty turnpike, and warned from casual deviation by advertisements which menace the summary vindication of the proprietor's monopoly of his extensive park, by spring-guns or man-traps, or the more protracted, yet scarce less formidable denunciation, of what is often, and scarce unjustly spelled, " *persecution* according to law." Above all, the peasant lives and dies as his fathers did, in the cot where he was born, without ever experiencing the horrors of a work-house. This may compensate for the want of much beef, beer, and pudding, in those to whom habit has not made this diet indispensable.

It is to be hoped that experimental legislation will pause ere consigning a race which is con-

tented with its situation to banishment, because
they only offer at present their hardy virtues
and industry to the stock of national prosperity,
instead of communicating largely to national
wealth. Even considered as absolute paupers,
they have some right to such slight support as
may be necessary to aid them in maintaining
themselves by their own industry. If the poor
elsewhere could be maintained without the degrading sense that they were receiving eleemo-
synary aid, it would be the better for themselves and their country.

I will admit, for argument's sake, that the
public funds which have established those fishing stations might have been bestowed to better
advantage; still, having been so expended, we
ought certainly not to be hasty in withdrawing
our support, even if we may judge that it was
incautiously granted at first. The philosopher,
in the fanciful Tale of Frankenstein, acted un-
wisely in creating the unnatural being to which
art enabled him to give life and motion; but
when he had, like a second Prometheus, given
sensation and power of thought to the creation
of his skill and science, he had no title to desert

the giant whom he had called into existence ; and the story shows that no good came of his being discontented with his own handy-work. But I contend, that the establishments to which I allude exhibit nothing save what may render the founders and encouragers proud of the result of their patriotic labours.

I do therefore hope that the present contented and rapidly improving condition of so many fellow-creatures, will be considered as something in the scale, when a measure shall be finally weighed, which, in the opinion of all connected with the north of Scotland, threatens to deprive them of the means of livelihood.

On other national topics I have already said enough. Those who look only at states and ledgers, hold such feelings as arise upon points of national honour, as valueless as a cypher without a numeral prefixed. Right or wrong, however, they still have an effect on the people of Scotland, as all can bear witness who were here when his Majesty honoured the capital of his ancestors with his own presence. We would not plead these too high neither, nor cling tenaciously by antiquated pretensions, which may obstruct the general welfare of the empire ; but we deprecate that sort of change which is made for the mere sake of innovation. A proud nation cannot endure such experiments when they touch honour—a poor one cannot brook them when attended with heavy loss. We are all aware that many changes must of necessity be —the political atmosphere is heavy and gloomy with the symptoms of them,

" And coming events cast their shadows before."

These changes will be wrought in their time ; but we trust they will not be forced forward suddenly, or until the public mind is prepared for, and the circumstances of the country require them.

Seasonable improvements are like the timely and regular showers, which, falling softly and silently upon the earth, when fittest to be received, awaken its powers of fertility. Hasty innovation is like the headlong hurricane, which may indeed be ultimately followed by beneficial consequences, but is, in its commencement and immediate progress, attended by terror, tumult, and distress.

This is indeed a period when change of every kind is boldly urged and ingeniously supported, nay, finds support in its very singularity; as the wildest doctrines of enthusiasm have been often pleaded with most eloquence, and adopted with most zeal. One philosopher will convert the whole country into work-houses, just as Commodore Trunnion would have arranged each parish on the system of a man-of-war. Another class has turned the system of Ethics out of doors, and discovers on the exterior of the scull, the passions of which we used to look for the source within. One set of fanatics join to dethrone the Deity, another to set up Prince Hohenloe. The supporters of all find preachers, hearers, and zealots, and would find martyrs if persecuted. We are at such a speculative period obliged to be cautious in adopting measures which are supported only by speculative argument. Let men reason as ingeniously as they will, and we will listen to them, amused if we are not convinced. I have heard with great pleasure an ingenious person lecture on phrenology, and have been much interested in his process of reasoning. But should such a philosopher propose to saw off or file away any of the bumps on my scull, by way of improving the moral sense, I am afraid I should demur to the motion.

I have read, I think in Lucian, of two architects, who contended before the people at Athens which should be intrusted with the task of erecting a temple.   The first made a luminous oration, showing that he was, in theory at least, master of his art, and spoke with such glibness in the hard terms of architecture, that the assembly could scarce be prevailed on to listen to his opponent, an old man of unpretending appearance,   But when he obtained audience, he said in a few words, " All that this young man can talk of, I have DONE."   The decision was unanimously in favour of Experience against Theory.   This resembles exactly the question now tried before us.

Here stands Theory, a scroll in her hand, full of deep and mysterious combinations of figures, the least failure in any one of which may alter the result entirely, and which you must take on trust, for who is capable to go through and check them ? *There* lies before you a practical

System, successful for upwards of a century.
The one allures you with promises, as the saying goes, of untold gold,—the other appeals to
the miracles already wrought in your behalf.
The one shows you provinces, the wealth of
which has been tripled under her management,
—the other a problem which has never been
practically solved. Here you have a pamphlet
—there a fishing town—here the long-continued
prosperity of a whole nation—and there the
opinion of a professor of Economics, that in such
circumstances she ought not by true principles to
have prospered at all. In short, good countrymen, if you are determined, like Æsop's dog, to
snap at the shadow and lose the substance, you
had never such a gratuitous opportunity of ex-
changing food and wealth for moonshine in the
water.

Adieu, sir. This is the last letter you will receive from,

Yours, &c.

MALACHI MALAGROWTHER.

EDINBURGH:
Printed by James Ballantyne & Co.